ARCHANGELS

HOW TO INVOKE AND WORK WITH
ANGELIC MESSENGERS

ABOUT THE AUTHOR

Richard Webster was born and raised in New Zealand. He has been interested in the psychic world since he was nine years old. He became interested in angels in his mid-twenties when he started receiving messages from his guardian angel. He was concerned at first, as he had no idea where the words were coming from. Once he learned they came from his guardian angel, he started learning as much as he could about the subject and has now written nine books about angels.

Richard's first book was published in 1972, fulfilling a childhood dream of becoming an author. Richard is now the author of more than a hundred books and is still writing today. His bestselling books include *Spirit Guides & Angel Guardians* and *Creative Visualization for Beginners*.

Richard has appeared on several radio and TV programs in the United States and abroad. He currently resides in New Zealand with his wife and three children. He regularly travels the world to give lectures, hold workshops, and continue his research.

ARCHANGELS

HOW TO INVOKE & WORK WITH
ANGELIC MESSENGERS

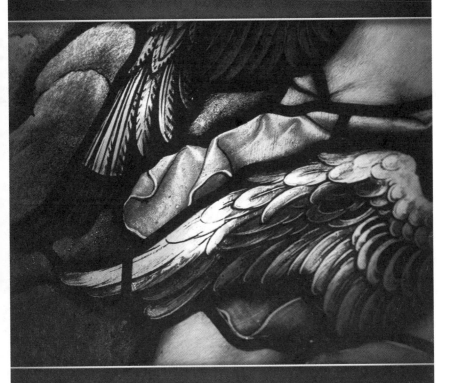

RICHARD WEBSTER

LLEWELLYN PUBLICATIONS
Woodbury, Minnesota

FIRST EDITION
First Printing, 2022

Cover design by Shannon McKuhen

Llewellyn Publications is a registered trademark of Llewellyn Worldwide Ltd.

Library of Congress Cataloging-in-Publication Data (Pending)
ISBN: 978-0-7387-7026-0

Llewellyn Publications
A Division of Llewellyn Worldwide Ltd.
2143 Wooddale Drive
Woodbury, MN 55125-2989
www.llewellyn.com

Printed in the United States of America

DEDICATION

For all the people who support my Contact Your Angels
page on Facebook. Thank you very much.

CONTENTS

INTRODUCTION

The word "archangel" is a combination of the words "arch" (meaning "chief") and "angel"; combined, the meaning is "chief angel." Consequently, archangels are angels of high status who possess great influence and power. For instance, archangel Gabriel is God's chief messenger, and archangel Michael is God's main warrior in the endless battle against evil.

"Archangel" as a title is commonly used to describe all angels of importance; until the Middle Ages, they were considered the most important angels of all. At that time, theologians became interested in creating different ranks of angels, so the archangels were demoted. Because of this, "archangel" also describes a rank of angels in the celestial hierarchy of angels.

There are usually thought to be seven archangels. In the book of Revelation, John wrote: "I saw the seven angels which stood before God" (Revelation 8:2). These seven are believed to be archangels, but no one knows the names of all seven. Over many years, different names and varying numbers of archangels have been suggested.

Only two archangels are mentioned by name in the Bible: Michael and Gabriel. The same two archangels are named in the Koran: Jibril (Gabriel) and Michael. Islam recognizes two other archangels as well: Azrael, the angel of death; and Israfel, the angel of music, who will blow the trumpet on Judgment Day.

The book of Enoch names seven archangels: Uriel, Raguel, Michael, Seraqael, Gabriel, Haniel, and Raphael. However, Judaism suggests Phanuel as a replacement for Uriel. Other sources claim that there are twelve archangels who are connected to the signs of the zodiac. The Kabbalah lists ten archangels, though the number is actually nine, as Metatron is listed twice.

Despite variations in the number of possible archangels, most authorities agree that the main tasks of archangels are to carry out the commands of God and to act as God's most important messengers. The most notable example of this occurred when Archangel Gabriel told Mary that she would give birth to Jesus. Archangels also look after empires, countries, cities, and other large groups of people. In addition, they act as guardian angels for highly-evolved people who have special spiritual work to perform in this incarnation.

In this book I discuss the angels who are most likely to be archangels, though it's inevitable that I'll miss some whom other people might consider to be archangels. It's worth noting that angels are not interested in their names or the particular choir or order to which humans say they belong. The archangels know their tasks and responsibilities, and they work hard to fulfil the wishes of the Divine.

I've also included a number of different ways to communicate with the archangels. I hope you'll contact the angels in this book that relate to your needs and allow them to help you.

ANGELS 101

P eople have believed in angels for thousands of years. Today, at a time when the world has become more and more secular, one would expect the number of believers to have declined. Interestingly, the opposite has occurred—more people believe in angels today than ever before. A December 2011 Associated Press—GfK poll found that 77 percent of Americans believe in angels (https://www.cbsnews.com/news/poll-nearly-8-in-10-americans-believe-in-angels/).

WHAT ANGELS ARE

In his 1966 book *The Christian Universe*, eminent theologian Eric Lionel Mascall (1905–1993) wrote: "Behind and beyond the physical universe, there is a realm of purely spiritual beings" (Mascall, 110). Angels are spiritual beings of pure light who operate on a different vibrational frequency to us. They exist solely to help God carry out his will (Tobit 12:18). John of Damascus (ca. 675–ca. 749 CE) wrote, "An angel, then, is an intelligent essence, in perpetual motion, with free will, incorporeal, ministering to God, having obtained by grave an immortal nature: and the Creator alone knows the form and limitation of its essence." The word "angel" comes from the Greek word *angelos*, which means "messenger."

Throughout history and in many religions, angels have conveyed messages to and from the Divine.

Angels are genderless and most frequently appear in human form. Angels seem to always appear in male form in the Bible and are considered masculine in the Jewish tradition. In the Bible, angels usually start the conversation by saying, "Fear not." In more modern times, angels appear in nonthreatening guises and consequently may appear as women, adolescents, and even children.

Angels protect and guide humankind, and usually appear when people are in desperate need of comfort or support. As they can appear in any shape or form they wish, it's possible for them to appear as butterflies, winged figures, rainbows, or bright lights. They can appear in dreams and be sensed in weather formations, such as rain and clouds. To appear in human form, however, they need to lower their vibrations to our level so that we are able to sense their presence and, in some cases, see them.

ANGEL SIGHTINGS

Throughout history, there have been numerous accounts of people who saw angels. Archangel Gabriel visited Mary to tell her she was going to give birth to Jesus. Gabriel made herself visible to Muhammad before dictating the Koran to him. Joan of Arc saw Archangel Michael. Dr. John Dee, astrologer to Queen Elizabeth I, saw Archangel Uriel flying past his home in Mortlake, near London. The English artist and poet William Blake saw a flock of angels in a tree while visiting Peckham Rye when he was just eight years old.

There are also a few instances of people who regularly saw angels. One striking example of this was Saint Frances of Rome (1384–1440), who saw an archangel every day for twenty-four years.

Born into a wealthy family, she announced at the age of eleven that she wanted to become a nun. Unfortunately her family had different ideas for her; one year later (when she was twelve), she was forced to marry Lorenzo Ponziani, commander of the papal troops in Rome. Despite being forced to marry, the marriage was a happy one and the couple had several children. In 1411, the couple's first son, Evangelista, was close to death. He told his mother that he could see the angels who had come to take him to heaven. He promised to remember his mother.

One year to the day after he died, Frances spent all night praying in the family's oratory. As dawn broke, the oratory was filled with a bright light, and Frances saw Evangelista standing next to another boy of about the same age. Both looked incredibly beautiful. Evangelista told his mother that he was in heaven and that his companion was an archangel who had been sent by God to look after her. He would remain with her, and she would always be able to see him with her eyes. Evangelista said that he had to return to heaven and that the archangel would always remind her of him. After saying that, Evangelista smiled and returned to heaven.

Frances fell at the feet of the archangel and gave thanks to God for this incredible blessing. As the brilliant light that emanated from the archangel was too strong for her eyes, she initially gazed at the light that surrounded him. When she was able to look at him directly, he appeared as a normal nine-year-old boy with a beautiful smile and sparkling eyes. He wore a white tunic and a gown that reached to his feet. His golden hair reached to his shoulders, and the light emanating from it was strong enough to enable Frances to read in the dark and walk through her home at night without needing a candle. Whenever the devil appeared, the archangel put the fear of God into him by shaking his hair. His hair also enabled Frances to read the secret thoughts of others.

After her husband died in 1436, Frances joined the Institute of Oblates as its most junior member, even though she herself had founded the order. On the day she joined the order, she had a vision in which her archangel was replaced by a member of the choir of powers. This angel remained with her for the final four years of her life (Parente, chapter 10).

In 1608, she was canonized, and in 1925 Pope Pius XI declared her the patron saint of automobile drivers, as a legend said that whenever Frances traveled, an angel lit the road ahead of her with a lantern. She is also the patron saint of widows. Members of the Benedictines honor her as the patron saint of oblates.

There have also been instances where angels were seen by some people but not by others who happened to be present. In the Bible is a story about a magician called Balaam who was riding a donkey when an angel blocked their way. The donkey saw the angel, but Balaam didn't, and he beat the donkey for refusing to move. It took Balaam several minutes before he was able to see the angel (Numbers 22:20–35).

ANGELS IN RELIGION

In the Christian tradition, the history of angels goes back to the first day of creation. In the apocryphal book of Jubilees, angels are said to have been created on the first day, after the heaven and earth but before the firmament (Jubilees 2:2). This meant that angels were able to help God with the rest of creation.

Around 3000 BCE, the ancient Sumerians believed in *anunnaki*, "creatures from the sky." The anunnaki were Divine messengers who had incredible powers (Black and Green, 93). They communicated messages between humans and the gods. The oldest known depiction of an angel is on a six-thousand-year-old Sumerian stele (stone column) that shows a winged figure pouring the water of life into a cup belonging to a king (Roland, [year] 12). There are many other depictions of winged beings that are thousands of years old. The Mesopotamians had griffins, huge winged figures that are part human and part animal. Egyptian mythology had Nepthys, twin sister of the goddess Isis, who enfolded the dead in her wings. The great Sphinx of Giza is said to be a monument to their great angel Hu (Humann, 88). Hermes, the winged Greek messenger of the gods, helped humans and carried messages.

The first monotheistic religion, Zoroastrianism, began in Persia somewhere between three and four thousand years ago when an angel called Vohu-Manah delivered a message from God to a Persian mystic called Zoroaster. Vohu-Manah was nine times the size of a human. With his help, Zoroaster was able to temporarily leave his body and experience the presence of Ahura Mazda, Lord of Light and Wisdom in addition to the many angels who surrounded him. Ahura Mazda taught Zoroaster everything he needed to know to become the first prophet of the new religion that would become Zoroastrianism. Ahura Mazda created six archangels called Amesha Spentas as well as a number of less important angels, including guardian angels. Zoroastrianism was possibly the world's first dualist belief system, as Ahura Mazda waged a constant battle against the forces of evil, led by Angra Mainyo, Lord of Evil and Destruction. Zoroastrianism was largely displaced in the region in the seventh century CE by the rise of Islam, but it is still practiced today in parts of Iran and India. Today, followers of Zoroastrianism in India are called Parsis. The beliefs of this religion had a huge influence on Judaism, Christianity, and Islam.

Judaism accepted angels into their cosmology, where Michael is considered the guardian angel of the Israelites. Raphael, Gabriel, and Uriel are also important angels in Judaism. A popular Jewish prayer includes all four archangels:

"May Michael, the protector of God, stand at my right hand; and Gabriel, the power of God, stand at my left; before me, Uriel, the light of God; and behind me, Raphael, the healing of God. And above my head, may there be the abiding presence of God, the Shekinah."

The Essenes, who wrote the Dead Sea Scrolls, believed in seven angels of the Earthly Mother. These were the angels of the sun, water, air, earth, life, joy, and the Earthly Mother. They also had seven angels of the Heavenly Father. These were the angels of power, love, wisdom, eternal life, creativity, peace, and the Heavenly Father.

Despite the large number of angelic appearances recorded in the Bible, it took Christianity hundreds of years to accept the reality of angels. In 325 CE, the First Ecumenical Council accepted that angels existed. This council even stated that Christians could ask angels to help them get to heaven. However, this was rescinded twenty years later when the Second Council decided that belief in angels would confuse people and hinder them from worshipping Christ. Finally, in 787 CE, the Seventh Ecumenical Synod accepted that angels were created to intercede between God and humankind.

Michael, Raphael, Gabriel, and Uriel are important angels in Christianity, as well as Judaism. Only three angels are mentioned by name in the Bible: Michael, Gabriel, and Lucifer. Two others are mentioned by name in the Apocrypha: Raphael in the book of Tobit, and Uriel in the book of Esdras. Except for Lucifer, all of these are archangels. Lucifer was also an archangel but was banished to hell after leading a battle against God in heaven.

Belief in angels is one of the six articles of faith in Islam. It was Jibril (the archangel Gabriel) who revealed the Koran, the holy book of Islam, to Muhammad. Jibril also visited Muhammad in Mecca and flew with him to Jerusalem, where they spoke with Abraham, Moses, Jesus, John the Baptist, and other prophets. After that, they climbed a ladder to heaven where Jibril introduced him to God.

An angel was also responsible for the founding of the Church of Latter-Day Saints. On September 21, 1823, an angel called Moroni appeared to a young man called Joseph Smith, and told him to go to a hill in New York state where a number of gold plates containing the Book of Mormon would be found. Joseph Smith found the plates but wasn't able to move them. Moroni appeared again and told him that it was too soon to retrieve the plates and translate them from Hebrew into English. Joseph waited patiently for four years before he could retrieve and translate them. Once he had done that, Moroni returned and carried the plates back to heaven.

Joseph Smith believed that certain gifted people could become angels after they died. In Mormonism, Adam, the first man, is believed to be Archangel Michael, and Noah is now Archangel Gabriel.

There are no angels in Hinduism, though they have spirit beings called *devas* or "shining ones" who live on a higher plane than humanity. Their task is to protect, motivate, and encourage humankind.

Devas also feature in Buddhism, in which they are spiritual beings who appear as emanations of light. They play no direct role in the activities of humankind but rejoice whenever a good deed is performed anywhere in the world.

RESEARCH INTO ANGELS

Throughout the centuries, leading scholars and theologians have continued to study angels. In the Middle Ages, Italian Dominican friar and philosopher Saint Thomas Aquinas (1225–1274) suggested that angels were made of pure spirit but could assume human or any other form they wished whenever necessary. Thomas Aquinas was known as the angelic doctor and in his major work, *Summa Theologica*, he answered 118 specific questions about angels. And in his other book, *Summa Contra Gentiles*, he included eight proofs to convince people to believe in angels. One of these was that the human soul continues to live after the death of the physical body. Consequently, angels can live without bodies and are already in the state that human beings ultimately become (Aquinas, 312–316).

There are many stories about Thomas Aquinas, including a strange legend about his mother's attempts to prevent him from joining the Dominicans when he was nineteen years old. She arranged for his brothers to kidnap him, and he was kept securely in the family castle for more than a year. While he was there, his brothers sent a young woman to seduce him. Thomas rejected her advances and sent her away. Before his family could try anything else, two angels visited Thomas and placed a magic girdle around his hips to protect him from any further temptation.

The other major philosopher-theologian of the time, John Duns Scotus (ca. 1265–1308), thought that angels were made of finer material than human beings, which is why they were invisible. However, they had the ability to make themselves visible to humans whenever there was a reason to do so.

In the sixteenth century, Dr. John Dee (1527–1608), the alchemist, astrologer, and magician, engaged in lengthy sessions with Edward Kelley, a scryer, to transcribe the secret language that angels used to communicate. It sounds fanciful, but the Enochian language they decoded has its own syntax and grammar and was eventually adopted by the Hermetic Order of the Golden Dawn in the late nineteenth century. More people are studying and using it today than ever before.

Swedish scientist and mystic Emmanuel Swedenborg (1688–1772), was a well-known and reputable scientist when, in his middle fifties, he started writing books about his experiences with angels. Because of his reputation, his accounts of angelic communication were accepted by many people. In those accounts, he explained that angels were invisible because they weren't made of matter but that it was possible for humans to see them by developing their intuition. Swedenborg wrote many books on theology with the help of the angels he talked with every day. His books are still available—and despite some contradictions—contain comprehensive descriptions of his view of the angelic kingdom.

Austrian philosopher and mystic Rudolf Steiner (1865–1925) began using clairvoyance to communicate with nature spirits and angels when he was a child. He believed that angels were water spirits who influenced human beings. Archangels were fire spirits who influenced large groups of people. Steiner thought that above these were archai, universal spirits who oversaw humanity as a whole.

Karl Barth (1886–1968), a Swiss theologian, started working on his thirteen-volume *Church Dogmatics* in 1932 and continued writing it for the rest of his life. In it, he discussed angels in great detail. He believed that angels bring heaven down to earth, and when they speak, it is actually God talking to us. Likewise, when they act, it is God who is acting. Barth believed that angels were above us, as they're able to witness God at work. However, at the same time, they were below us, as God's work was directed toward people rather than the angelic kingdom. He wrote: "To deny the angels is to deny God himself" (Barth, 486).

Research into angels is still continuing today. One modern day researcher came up with a highly controversial idea about angels. This was Dr. Geddes MacGregor (1909–1998), a distinguished author and professor of philosophy, who suggested that angels could be a highly developed race of extraterrestrials (MacGregor, 57).

You don't need to be an academic to explore the angelic kingdom. Today, more and more people are establishing their own personal connections with angels and are deriving significant benefits from it. Angels help in many different ways, among them helping people realize that they are part of God and are conducting a divine mission in this incarnation. Irish mystic Lorna Byrne, author of the 2008 international bestseller *Angels in My Hair,* sees angels as clearly as she sees people and talks with them every day. Angels play an important role in every aspect of her life, and her books have introduced many people to the angelic realms.

In the following chapters we'll discuss the hierarchy of angels before moving on to the archangels and their importance in the celestial realms. We'll start with the four major archangels—Raphael, Michael, Gabriel, and Uriel—and then have a look at lesser-known archangels. Finally, we'll cover a variety of ways to communicate and work with the different archangels to help you achieve your goals and develop a closer connection with the Divine.

THE HIERARCHY OF ANGELS

T he hierarchy of angels was developed by a number of important scholars, including Saint Jerome, Saint Ambrose, and Saint Gregory, in Christianity's early years. The hierarchy of angels played an important role in Christianity and Judaism but has never been adopted by other religions.

All organizations of any size have a hierarchy of people ranked one above another according to their status and authority. A business hierarchy looks like a pyramid, with the CEO at the top and the most junior members of the organization at the bottom. In fact, the word "hierarchy" originally meant the ranking of angels into three divisions of nine orders. The angels at the top of the pyramid were those closest to God, and the ones at the bottom were closest to humankind. A number of hierarchies were proposed, but the one that gained most acceptance was devised by Pseudo-Dionysius, who lived in the late fifth and early sixth centuries CE. It was Pseudo-Dionysius who coined the word "hierarchy" from two Greek words: *hieros* ("sacred") and *arkhia* ("rule"). He wrote that a hierarchy was "a sacred order, a state of understanding and an activity approximating as closely as possible to the Divine" (Pseudo-Dionysius, 153). He also wrote: "The goal of a hierarchy is to enable beings to be as like as possible to God and to be at one with him" (154).

No one knows who Pseudo-Dionysius was, though he is likely to have been a Syrian monk. He claimed in his writings to be Saint Dionysius the Areopagite, who was converted to Christianity by Saint Paul (Acts 17:34) and later became the first bishop of Athens, dying as a Christian martyr. However, Pseudo-Dionysius lived many centuries after the person he claimed to be. He probably thought his ideas would achieve greater acceptance if he used a pseudonym. Although some people had doubts about the veracity of the author from the beginning, it wasn't until the sixteenth century that people started openly questioning his authenticity. Until the twentieth century, most people believed Pseudo-Dionysius's writings were written by the real Saint Dionysius.

Pseudo-Dionysius listed and explained his hierarchy in *The Celestial Harmony*, a book that was hugely influential for well over a thousand years. In this book, he used the traditional nine orders of angels that were mentioned by name in the Bible and placed them into three groups of three, known as triads. Each of the three ranks of angels in each triad was then classified into three levels of intelligences. The top level is union or perfection, the second is illumination, and the third is purification. This system allowed the divine spirit to descend into the world, and also enabled humans to reach up to heaven.

This system can be visualized by having God at the center, encircled by nine orders of angels. Every angel possesses the powers and capabilities of the angels below it in the hierarchy, but not the abilities of the angels above it.

PSEUDO–DIONYSIS'S HIERARCHY OF ANGELS

Triad One: The Angels Closest to God

Seraphim

The name "seraphim" comes from the Hebrew word *sarap*, which means "the burning one." The seraphim are angels of fire and light who can purify people with a flash of lightning. Their divine, flaming light is so strong that not even members of the cherubim (ranked one below the seraphim) can look at them. Apparently, Saint Francis of Assisi saw a seraph and received his stigmata from it. This was the first time that a human being received a stigmata, which are the marks resembling the wounds Jesus received when he was crucified. Isaiah and Saint Francis are the only human beings to have seen a seraph. According to Isaiah, seraphs have six wings (Isaiah 6:1), and the members of the choir of seraphim worship God unceasingly, twenty-fours a day, by calling out, "Holy, holy, holy, is the Lord of hosts; the whole earth is full of his glory" (Isaiah 6:3). These words, known as the Kadosh, are still used in Jewish services today.

At the time when Pseudo-Dionysius was writing his books, it made sense to have the Divine encircled by endlessly singing members of the seraphim. It's more likely that they surround the Divine and send out pure, intense love and positive energy to the entire universe.

Before the war in heaven, Satan was the most highly ranked member of the seraphim. Ezekiel wrote: "Thus saith the Lord God; thou sealest up the sum, full of wisdom, and perfect in beauty" (Ezekiel 28:12). Ezekiel also wrote: "Thou wast perfect in thy ways from the day that thou wast created, till iniquity was found in thee" (Ezekiel 28:15).

The ruling princes of the seraphim are: Michael, Seraphiel, Jehoel, Uriel, Kemuel, Metatron, and Nathanael.

Cherubim

The name *"cherubim"* is derived from the Hebrew word *kerub*, which means "fullness of knowledge." Pseudo-Dionysius wrote that the name "cherubim" signified "the power to know and to see God" (Pseudo-Dionysius, 205C). Artists usually depict the cherubim with multi-eyed peacock's feathers to symbolize their powers of observation and knowledge. The cherubim look after the sun, the moon, and the stars. They're also responsible for looking after the heavenly records and helping people gain knowledge and divine wisdom. As well as helping people learn new skills, they also spend much of their time teaching the lower orders of angels.

The ruling princes of the cherubim are: Gabriel, Cherubiel, Ophanael, Raphael, Uriel, and Zophiel.

Thrones

The thrones are often called wheels, and artists depict them as large fiery wheels with four wings completely covered with penetrating eyes. This is how the prophet Ezekiel saw them in his vision (Ezekiel 1:1–28). The thrones are the wheels of the chariot throne of God. The thrones are always in the presence of God and continually sing glorias to him.

The thrones are angels of justice and administer divine justice to humankind to maintain the universal laws of the universe. They also act as God's advisers, and advise him whenever important decisions need to be made. The thrones look after all planets and solar systems. The thrones are peaceful, calm, healing, and supportive. Many people believe that the Virgin Mary is a member of the choir of thrones.

The ruling princes of the thrones are: Orifiel, Zaphkiel, Zabkiel, Jophiel, and Raziel.

Triad Two: The Princes or Leaders of the Heavenly Kingdom

Dominions

The dominions, sometimes known as dominations, are thought to be the oldest angels. Their main task is to supervise the angels below them in the hierarchy to ensure that the universe works the way it should. The seraphim, cherubim, and thrones in the first triad do not need supervision. The dominions are natural leaders and mediators who inspire other angels by their example. They are usually depicted wearing green and gold robes and two wings. They carry a staff with a cross on top of it in their left hands, and a seal bearing a monogram of Jesus in their right hand. These are symbols of their power and authority. Archdeacon Boudon wrote that it was: "The special office of these spirits of light to make known to us the commands of God; they are, so to say, the secretaries of state of the great King Jesus" (Boudon, 144).

The ruling princes of the dominions are: Zadkiel, Hashmal, Zachariel, and Muriel.

Virtues

The virtues are in charge of nature and all the natural laws of the universe, such as the seasons. According to Hebrew tradition, they're also responsible for the miracles that go against these laws. Saint Gregory the Great (540–604) believed that God performed most of his miracles with the help of the virtues. The virtues enjoy working with positive, go-getting people who do the best they can to help all humanity. They help heroes, as well as people who need courage and help in handling life. Virtues are usually depicted by artists as bishops carrying a lily or a red rose to symbolize the passion of Christ. They wear a golden belt around their waists. The two men in "white apparel" who accompanied Jesus when he ascended into heaven are believed to be members of the order of virtues (Acts 1:10). According to the book of Adam and Eve, two virtues and twelve angels helped Eve when she was pregnant with Cain (Charles, xxi, 1).

The ruling princes of the virtues are: Uzziel, Gabriel, Michael, Peliel, Barbiel, Sabriel, Hanael, Hamaliel, and Tarshish.

Powers

This order gained its name from the fact that they possess powers well beyond those of human beings. The powers prevent demons and other spirits from attempting to overthrow the world. Because they are courageous, they guard the pathways into heaven. They also look after the Akashic records and protect people's souls. Artists usually portray them as large, powerful men wearing armor and holding chained demons. They sometimes hold a golden staff in their right hands.

The ruling princes of the powers are: Camael, Gabriel, and Verchiel.

Triad Three: The Ministering Angels

Principalities

The principalities look after large groups, such as continents, countries, cities, towns, and sacred places. They are good administrators who are constantly involved in governing the universe (Romans 8:38; Ephesians 1:21, 3:10, 6:12; Colossians 1:16, 2:10, 2:15). They also guide religious leaders of all faiths and encourage guardian angels in their work. Artists usually draw angels of the principalities as soldiers, wearing armor and crowns. They also frequently carry a cross, a scepter, or a sword.

The ruling princes of the principalities are: Nisroc, Hanael, Requel, Cerviel, and Amael.

Archangels

Archangels are God's most important messengers, though sending messages is only a small part of what they do. They also direct the will of God and control the seasons, the movement of the stars, the waters of the earth, and all life on earth. They also supervise the guardian angels. They transmit divine love to all angels, regardless of their relative position in the hierarchy.

Michael and Gabriel are the only members of the choir of archangels to be mentioned by name in the Bible. The apostle John wrote that he saw "seven angels who stood before God" (Revelation 8:2). Traditionally, these angels are believed to be the seven archangels, and a number of angels have been suggested for these roles. The word "archangel" is mentioned on two occasions in the Bible. Michael is described as "Michael the archangel" in Jude 9, and "For the Lord himself will descend from heaven with a shout, with the voice of the archangel, and with the trump[et] of God" (1 Thessalonians 4:16). In the apocryphal book of Tobit, Raphael told Tobias that he was one of the seven angels who stand before the throne of God (Tobit 12:15). Some authorities say Raphael is head of the choir of archangels.

The ruling princes of the archangels are: Metatron, Raphael, Michael, Gabriel, Barbiel, Jehudiel, and Barachiel.

Angels

The angels in this group are the ones closest to human beings. If the seraphim are generals, the angels are privates in God's army.

They're sometimes described as the worker bees of the angelic world. Angels from this group are the ones humans are most likely to see, and most guardian angels come from this choir (though it is possible for guardian angels to come from any choir). Guardian angels are assigned to a person and look after him or her through every incarnation. There are millions of angels in this group.

The ruling princes of the choir of angels are: Phaleg, Adnachiel, Gabriel, and Chayyliel.

PROBLEMS WITH THE HIERARCHY OF ANGELS

The most obvious difficulty with the hierarchy of angels is that archangels are ranked so low on the list. The "arch" part of their name comes from the Greek *archein*, which means "most important" or "original." One would assume that archangels were possibly the most important angels of all. Seeing them listed as the second-to-last choir of angels prompted the theologian Geddes MacGregor (1909–1998) to write: "Mightn't it be almost like having a corporal in charge of the United States Army?" (MacGregor, 79.)

Pseudo-Dionysius may have believed that the most important angels spent their time in contemplation and prayer and were not involved in the everyday concerns of human beings. Consequently, he placed the most important groups closest to God, while the less important angels were placed nearer to humankind. Archangels and angels are normally the only angels visible to us, so it may be because of this proximity that archangels were placed immediately above the angels. Archangels fare much better in the Greek Testament of Levi, part of a manuscript called the *Testaments of the Twelve Patriarchs*. In Levi's account, God and the archangels live together in the highest heaven (Charles, 3:3–6).

There are other complications. Archangel Michael is considered to be captain of the host of the Lord, which makes him arguably the most important angel of all. This placement occurred because initially there were only two groups: angels and archangels. Ultimately, the angelic hierarchy is a human construct; over the years, people have come up with many different ways of classifying them in to different groups.

Another problem that wasn't considered back in the sixth century CE was that God apparently created vast numbers of angels who spent all their time in praise. Humans are encumbered and limited by their egos, but I'm certain the Divine has no need for anything like that.

Yet another problem is that Pseudo-Dionysius' hierarchy lasted as long as it did. In the thirteenth century, Thomas Aquinas gave it new life by accepting it uncritically, and even Rudolf Steiner did the same in the twentieth century. However, John Calvin (1509–1564), the founder of the Presbyterian Church, wrote that any conversations about the angelic hierarchies were "the vain babblings of idle men."

Angels, of course, go about their tasks blissfully unaware or unconcerned that humans have slotted them into nine categories. This doesn't impede them in their work, and they're able to instantly communicate and work with angels in any of the choirs whenever necessary.

In the next chapter we'll look more closely at archangels and what they do.

What Are Archangels?

In the Bible, Michael is the only angel identified as an archangel (Jude 9). He is also called "one of the chief princes" (Daniel 10:13), denoting his importance. Archangels are important angels who are actively involved in ensuring the well-being of every form of life on earth. Each archangel has a specific role to play in this.

Archangels have played a significant role in the history of religion. The "angel of the Lord" appears some sixty-five times in the Old Testament of the Bible. Although this angel is never identified, he or she is obviously important, and may well be an archangel. The first appearance of the angel of the Lord occurred when Hagar, Abraham's mistress, became pregnant and fled from the wrath of Abraham's wife, Sarah. The angel of the Lord found Hagar beside a spring on the road to Shur and told her to return to her mistress. The angel also told her that she was to call her son Ishmael (Genesis 16:11). Later, Hagar again found herself in the desert with her baby after being ordered out of Abraham's home. She had run out of water and placed her baby under a shrub. She moved a short distance away so that she wouldn't see Ishmael die. The angel of the Lord spoke to her again and told her that Ishmael would form "a great nation." After this, "God opened her eyes" and she saw a well of water that enabled her to feed her baby and herself (Genesis 21:17).

One of the most famous biblical stories about angels concerns Abraham, his son, Isaac, and the angel of God. God tested Abraham by telling him he had to sacrifice his son. He was told he had to take his son to the top of a remote mountain three days' walk away, and cut his throat using the same method he used when sacrificing a lamb. The blood would have to spill as an offering to prove his love of God. If Abraham was willing to sacrifice that which he loved more than anything else, it would prove that his devotion to God was absolute.

Surprisingly, Abraham didn't question this order. He sharpened his knife, collected wood, and without telling his wife what he was going to do, set off with Isaac, two servants, and an ass. At the foot of the mountain, he told the servants to look after the ass and to stay where they were and wait for him. After this, he and Isaac started climbing the mountain. At some stage, Isaac asked his father where they'd find the sacrificial lamb. Abraham replied, "My son, God will provide himself a lamb for a burnt offering." When they arrived at the spot that God had told him about, Abraham and Isaac built an altar and prepared a fire. When the fire was going, Abraham bound his son and placed him on the altar. He then picked up the knife to slay his son.

At this moment "the angel of the Lord" called to him from heaven: "Lay not thine hand upon the lad, neither do thou any thing unto him: for now I know that thou fearest God, seeing thou hast not withheld thy son, thine only son from me."

Abraham looked up and saw a ram caught in a thicket by his horns. With what must have been an unbelievable amount of relief, he sacrificed the sheep instead of his son.

The angel of the Lord then blessed Abraham by saying: "I will bless thee, and in multiplying I will multiply thy seed as the stars of the heavens, and as the sand which is upon the sea shore; and thy seed shall possess the gate of his enemies. And in thy seed shall all the nations of the earth be blessed; because thou hast obeyed my voice" (Genesis 22:1–18).

According to Jewish legend, Zadkiel was the archangel called "the angel of the Lord" who featured in the biblical account of the story of Abraham and Isaac. Artists usually depict Zadkiel holding a knife in reference to this. However, over the years, Michael and several other angels have also been credited with telling Abraham to release his son.

The angel of the Lord also helped the people of Israel as they were being chased by the Egyptian army. Exodus 14:19–20 says: "and the angel of God, which went before the camp of Israel, removed and went behind them; and the pillar of the cloud went from before their face, and stood behind them. And it came between the camp of the Egyptians and the camp of Israel; and it was a cloud and darkness to them, but it gave light by night to these: so that the one came not near the other all the night."

Archangel Gabriel is considered to be God's most important messenger. Two of his most important messages were recorded in the Gospel according to Luke. Archangel Gabriel visited a priest named Zacharias, and his wife Elisabeth, to tell them that they were to have a son, whom they were to name John. The couple were delighted but were also surprised, as they were both advanced in age. Zacharias queried the news, and was struck dumb until the baby was born (Luke 1:5–25). Elisabeth gave birth to a healthy baby who grew up to become John the Baptist.

Six months after visiting Zacharias and Elisabeth, Archangel Gabriel visited Mary, Elisabeth's cousin, to tell her that she'd give birth to Jesus. This event is called the Annunciation, and is the most important angelic visitation of all as far as Christians are concerned (Luke 1:26–38). Gabriel greeted Mary by saying: "Hail, thou that art highly favoured, the Lord is with thee: blessed art thou among women." Mary was troubled to be greeted in this way, and wondered what sort of greeting this could be. Gabriel continued: "Fear not, Mary: for thou hast found favour with God. And, behold, thou shalt conceive in thy womb, and bring forth a son, and shalt call his name JESUS. He shall be great, and shall be called the Son of the Highest: and the Lord God shall give unto him the throne of his father David: And he shall reign over the house of Jacob for ever; and of his kingdom there shall be no end." After a brief discussion, Mary said: "Behold the handmaid of the Lord; be it unto me according to thy word" (Luke 1:27–38).

Not surprisingly, Joseph, Mary's husband, wasn't happy with the situation and was concerned that it would bring disgrace to the family. An angel of the Lord appeared to him in a dream and said: "Joseph, thou son of David, fear not to take unto thee Mary thy wife: for that which is conceived in her is of the Holy Ghost. And she shall bring forth a son, and thou shalt call his name JESUS: for he shall save his people from their sins" (Matthew 1:20–21).

When Jesus was born, the angel of the Lord appeared to shepherds who were watching over their flock at night, to tell them the news of the birth of "a Saviour, which is Christ the Lord" (Luke 2:8–11).

In the Acts of the Apostles, the angel of the Lord rescued the apostle Peter from his prison cell. King Herod had arrested Peter and placed him under heavy guard in prison. One night, while Peter was sleeping between two soldiers who were shackled to him and with sentries guarding the entrance to the cell, the angel of the Lord appeared. A light appeared in the cell, and the angel struck Peter on the side and woke him up. "Arise up quickly," the angel said, and the chains immediately fell from Peter's hands. The angel told Peter to get dressed, and then the angel led him out of the prison. The Bible says that Peter didn't believe it was actually happening, thinking instead it was a vision. When they reached the large iron prison gate, it opened by itself, and they were able to leave the prison. Only then did Peter realize it wasn't a dream, and knew without a doubt that God had sent the angel to help him.

Now that he was free, Peter went to "the house of Mary the mother of John, whose surname was Mark; where many were gathered together praying" (Acts 12:12). The servant who answered Peter's knock on the door recognized his voice but was so happy she ran to tell everyone who was there, forgetting in her excitement to let him in. No one believed her. They told her she was mad, and that it was probably his angel (guardian angel). Peter had to continue knocking on the door until they opened it, after which he was able to tell "them how the Lord had brought him out of the prison" (Acts 12:17). Peter then went to a safe place where Herod's men wouldn't be able to find him. The following morning, after Herod's men had made a thorough search for him, Herod had the soldiers who were guarding him executed.

This is an interesting story, as Luke recorded it less than thirty years after it had happened. Luke is considered to be an honest and reliable historian, and his account of the incident also included a great deal of detail that was able to be verified from public sources. These included Peter's escape from prison, the execution of the guards, and the names of some of the people present, such as Mary, the mother of John, whose surname was Mark. It also included the embarrassing disbelief of the Christians who were present and actually praying for Peter's release at the time he knocked on the door. Peter himself believed he was seeing a vision until he discovered he was free. As one of Jesus's disciples, the reason Peter was imprisoned in the first place was for telling people about Jesus. It seems unlikely that he would lie about what happened, especially as the story didn't show him in the best light, given his initial disbelief that he was being rescued.

Archangels are the most powerful angels that human beings usually contact. It's rare for someone to contact one of the angels closest to God, such as a seraph or a member of the cherubim, for instance. Humans usually call on a specific archangel or angel, such as their guardian angel. When archangels appear to people, their first message is one that people should not be afraid. The reason for this is that when angels appear unexpectedly, they create fear and awe in the hearts of the people who see them. The vibrations of archangels are also extremely intense; Daniel lost consciousness when Archangel Gabriel appeared to him (Daniel 8:15–19). Archangels usually dampen their vibrations before making themselves visible. They frequently appear as people, and it is only later that they're recognized for who they are.

HOW MANY ARCHANGELS ARE THERE?

Traditions vary, but there have always been four or seven archangels. The four archangels are usually listed as Raphael, Michael, Gabriel, and Uriel. In the book of Enoch, Uriel is replaced by Phanuel (Laurence, 45). However, as Phanuel is often thought to be another name for Uriel, it's possible that both Uriel and Phanuel are the same angel.

Seven archangels are recognized in Judaism and Christianity. The first four are Michael, Raphael, Gabriel, and Uriel, but the remaining three have been debated and discussed for at least two thousand years. Here are a few of the angels who have been suggested for the last three positions: Anael, Aniel, Barchiel, Chamael, Jeduhiel, Jophiel, Metatron, Raguel, Raziel, Remiel, Sariel, Simael, Zadkiel, and Zaphiel.

In Islam, three of these archangels remain the same, though their names change slightly and become Israfil (Raphael), Mikha'il (Michael), and Jibril (Gabriel). In Islam, the fourth archangel is Azra'il (Azrael), the angel of death. Muslims say that Allah sent the four archangels to each corner of the world to gather the dust to create Adam, but Azra'il was the only one who succeeded, hence why human beings are mortal.

There are many lists of seven archangels, probably because seven is considered a holy number and the Bible says that seven princes saw the king's (God's) face (Esther 1:14). In addition to this, seven was the number of planets known to people in the ancient world.

Possibly the earliest list appeared in the twentieth chapter of the book of Enoch: Michael, Gabriel, Raphael, Uriel, Raguel, Saraqael, and Remiel. The book of Enoch was written between the third century BCE and the first century BCE, and this earlier list includes Uriel, who was replaced by Phanuel in the later list of four archangels which appeared in the fortieth chapter. (Rees, 242).

Here are a few other lists of the seven archangels:

Pseudo-Dionysius: Michael, Gabriel, Raphael, Uriel, Chamuel, Jophiel, and Zadkiel.

Testament of Solomon: Mikael, Gabriel, Uriel, Sabriel, Ariel, Iaoth, and Adonael.

Christian Gnostics: Michael, Gabriel, Raphael, Uriel, Barachiel, Sealtiel, and Jehudiel.

Gregory the Great: Michael, Gabriel, Raphael, Uriel, Simiel, Orifiel, and Zachariel.

Early in the twelfth century, a leading rabbi in Barcelona named Judah ben Barzillai constructed a list of twelve archangels, connecting each of them to different signs of the zodiac (Rees, 140).

Many people interested in New Age spirituality today also believe there are twelve archangels. Naturally, Michael, Raphael, Gabriel, and Uriel are included, along with Metatron. In addition to them, a wide variety of angels have been nominated, including: Anthriel, Aquariel, Barbiel, Barchiel, Chamuel, Jehudiel, Jophiel, Omniel, Perpetiel, Valoel, and Zadkiel.

TRADITIONAL ROLES OF THE ARCHANGELS

Throughout history, archangels have had five important roles. The most important of these is carrying messages between the Divine and humankind. Archangel Gabriel is the most important of these. She is close to God and is always available to transport messages to and from people. According to David the psalmist, Gabriel is one of "his angels, that excel in strength, that do his commandments, hearkening into the voice of his word" (Psalm 103:20).

Archangels also play an important role in looking after groups of people, such as empires and entire countries. An ancient Jewish tradition says that Michael is the guardian angel of Israel, and there are two biblical references to this. "Behold, I send an Angel before thee, to keep thee in the way, and to bring thee into the place which I have prepared" (Exodus 23:20). The angel is not identified as Michael in this passage, but is mentioned by name in Daniel 10:13: "but, lo, Michael, one of the chief princes, came to help me."

Archangels reveal celestial secrets to humanity. Whenever the time is right, the Divine uses archangels to deliver important information to people. Archangels protect, guide, and assist humanity in many different ways, and they also supervise guardian angels.

Because they're so close to humanity, archangels are uniquely willing to help us in any way they can and will respond immediately to our calls. You can ask them to help others, as well. Archangels are tireless and can appear in more than one place at a time. You can call on any of the archangels for help and support whenever necessary and be confident that they will instantly come to your aid.

In the next chapter, we'll look at the four most famous archangels: Michael, Raphael, Gabriel, and Uriel.

CHAPTER FOUR

THE FOUR MAIN ARCHANGELS

M ichael, Raphael, Gabriel, and Uriel are the best-known archangels. In this chapter, we'll cover the history of each of
these four archangels, and when to ask them for help. There's also a
guided visualization for each of them.

MICHAEL
"Who is like God"
Color: Blue, purple, gold

Michael is considered the greatest angel of all in the Christian, Jewish, and Islamic traditions. He's the only archangel mentioned by
name in the religious texts of all three religions. In the Bible he
is called "one of the chief princes" (Daniel 10:13) and "the great
prince" (Daniel 12:1).

Artists normally depict Michael with a sword, the scales of justice, and/or a blue flame of protection. Often this blue flame surrounds the sword. Many Renaissance paintings show him wearing
armor. These symbols all relate to Michael's courage, strength,
integrity, and willingness to provide protection. He gives these
qualities to people who call on him. He also provides patience,
sympathy, ambition, and motivation.

Michael is in charge of God's army, constantly fighting against the forces of evil. When Lucifer refused to bow down and worship God, Michael was asked to cast him and his followers out of heaven. The story of this epic battle can be found in the Bible (Revelation 12:7–17).

God rewarded Michael for his success in this battle by allowing him to receive immortal souls as they arrived in heaven. He weighs the souls to balance their good and bad deeds. Those with more good deeds than bad are allowed into heaven and are presented to God. The other souls are sent to purgatory.

According to the Gnostics, the seven great archangels created the universe for God, and were consequently there at the moment the universe began. The apocryphal Gospel of Bartholomew tells how God created man from clay that Michael had collected from the four corners of the earth.

Michael was not mentioned by name in the Bible until the book of Daniel, the twenty-seventh book of the Old Testament. However, according to Jewish legend, Michael and Gabriel served as witnesses at Adam and Eve's wedding. Michael is also believed to have visited Abraham and Sarah, wrestled with Jacob, and guided Moses and the children of Israel during their long trek through the wilderness. According to the apocryphal book of Adam and Eve, Michael helped Adam after he was expelled from the Garden of Eden. He also taught Adam how to farm, and even gave him a tour of heaven. After Adam's death, it was Michael who persuaded God to let his soul enter heaven. According to Jewish legend, Michael prevented Abraham from sacrificing his son Isaac. He also appeared to Moses in a burning bush, freed Peter from prison, and rescued Daniel from the lion's den. Some authorities say he proclaimed the Ten Commandments on Mount Sinai (Rees, 145).

According to legend, Michael was the guardian of Jesus and the Virgin Mary during their earthly lifetimes. According to the same legend, Jesus Christ asked Michael to tell his mother of her impending death and to look after her soul when it left her body (Jameson, 140). Because of this, Michael is sometimes called the Christian angel of death. Before someone dies, Michael appears and gives the soul an opportunity to redeem itself. This frustrates Satan and his helpers.

An important vision of Michael occurred in southern Italy in 492 CE. A wealthy man named Calgano owned a large number of cattle who fed on the side of a mountain. One day, a bull strayed, so Calgano summoned his men to find it. The bull was found at the top of the mountain by the entrance to a cave. Calgano was angry about the amount of time that had been wasted and asked one of his men to kill it. The servant fired an arrow at the bull. Miraculously, the arrow turned around in midflight and went straight into the heart of the man who had shot it, killing him.

Calgano and his servants were upset at what happened and asked a local bishop for advice. After the bishop had fasted and prayed for three days, Michael appeared to him in a vision and said that the man had been killed because the site was sacred to him, and that he wanted a church to be built there in his honor.

When the bishop, Calgano, and his men visited the cave, they found three altars inside, one adorned with an embroidered crimson and gold altar cloth. A stream of water sprang out from a rock and was found to have healing qualities. Naturally, a church was erected on the site and quickly became a popular place of pilgrimage. The cave is known as the Celestial Basilica, and people still visit it today to admire the beautiful marble statue of Michael, carved by Sansovino (Gittings, 102).

In 590 CE, a severe plague ravaged the city of Rome. It killed Pope Pelagius II, and the new pope, Gregory I (later to become Saint Gregory the Great), led a procession of citizens through the streets of the city. After three days, the procession reached the Tomb of Hadrian. Gregory saw Michael standing on top of the monument, casually sheathing a sword that was dripping with blood. This told Gregory that the plague was over, and he erected a church at the site which he dedicated to Michael. In 1752, Pope Benedict XIV had a large bronze statue of Michael placed on the tomb to commemorate this miraculous visitation.

In 706 CE, Aubert, Bishop of Avranches in France, had a vision in which Michael appeared to him. He told Aubert to visit the highest point of a large rock in Normandy that turned into an island at high tide. Michael said that he'd find a bull on the island and he was to build a church that covered the entire area that the bull had trampled with his hooves. He'd also find a spring of healing water there.

Aubert ignored the vision, thinking it was simply a strange dream. However, the dream occurred on two more occasions, and eventually Michael touched his forehead with his thumb, leaving a mark that remained there for the rest of the bishop's life. After this reinforcement, Aubert visited the island and built a small church on it. A more impressive church, built later, was finished by William the Conqueror. Over time, Mont-Saint-Michel became an important site for pilgrims to visit, and Michael was chosen as the patron saint of France. This patronage expanded to include England after William the Conqueror invaded it in 1066.

Joan of Arc (ca. 1412–1431) started hearing, and ultimately seeing, Michael from the age of thirteen. She saw him as a handsome young man, surrounded by other angels. Initially, his advice to her was to attend mass regularly and to lead a good, godly life. However, over time the message gradually changed and she came to believe that she could establish Charles VII as her country's rightful king. Michael gave her constant encouragement and even told her what flag she should use when leading her troops in her efforts to free France from English domination. The judges at her trial didn't believe her when she told them that Michael had walked on the ground (Barrett, 97). Joan of Arc was found guilty of heresy and burned at the stake in 1431. Her last words as the flames consumed her were to ask Michael to protect her as she moved on to the next life.

In 1884, Pope Leo XIII (1810–1903) fainted while attending a meeting with his cardinals. When he regained consciousness, he told the cardinals of a frightening vision he had seen of all the evil spirits who worked against the Church. Fortunately, Michael appeared and sent Satan and his helpers back to hell. The vision alarmed Pope Leo so much that he wrote a prayer, and ordered that it be recited at the end of mass to help protect the Church. This was made optional in the 1960s, but many people still gain comfort from saying it:

"St. Michael the Archangel, defend us in battle, keep us safe from the wickedness and snares of the devil. May God restrain him, we humbly pray, and do thou, O Prince of the Heavenly Host, by the power of God, cast Satan into hell, and all the evil spirits who prowl around the world seeking the ruin of souls. Amen."

Churches have been dedicated to Michael since the fourth century, and his feast day of September 29 has been celebrated since the ninth century. This day is called Michaelmas in the United Kingdom and many other countries. In 1950, the Roman Catholic Church canonized him, and made him Saint Michael. In this role he is the patron saint of grocers, sailors, doctors, police officers, and people in the armed forces.

When to Call on Archangel Michael

You can ask Archangel Michael for help and protection whenever you need it. Michael acts swiftly and will immediately be with you the instant you call out to him. The most common reason to request Michael's help is when you need physical protection, but he's available to provide spiritual, emotional, and mental protection as well.

Michael is ready to help whenever you need strength and courage for any reason. You might need physical strength to accomplish a particular task, or to handle severe pain. You might need emotional strength to help you deal with the unreasonable demands of someone close to you. You might need mental strength if the constant pressures and demands of your work are weighing you down. You might need Michael's strength and courage to enable you to overcome an addiction, or to take on a leadership role.

Archangel Michael can also help you find your inner truth and integrity to enable you to live according to your true nature.

Archangel Michael Guided Visualization

Guided visualizations are a highly effective way to explore the angelic realms and communicate with angels. You can work with creative visualizations in three different ways: You could record a suitable script, and then relax and listen to it. If you have a friend who is as interested in angels as you are, you could ask them to read the script to you, and you could reciprocate by having them relax while you read the script. The third method is to become familiar with what you want to do during the visualization and then relax and silently say the words to yourself. This third method is the most difficult, as our minds are easily distracted, making it hard to focus on the visualization. The best way is to start by recording a script and listening to that. Once you've become familiar with the process, you might like to practice the third method. This is the one I usually use, as I can do it at any time without needing any equipment.

Start by recording the script below for the Archangel Michael guided visualization. Once you've done that, set aside at least twenty minutes of time when you won't be disturbed. Temporarily switch off any phones. Make sure the room you are using is pleasantly warm, and wear clothes that are comfortable and loose-fitting. Sit down in a comfortable chair and close your eyes. Many people like to lie down when listening to guided visualizations. As I fall asleep easily, I prefer to sit in a recliner-type chair.

Here is the script:

"Take a nice deep breath in, and feel your eyelids relaxing as you exhale. Focus on your breathing and allow your body to relax more and more each time you exhale. It's a wonderful feeling to be able to relax and allow all the cares of the day to fade away as you drift down, deeper and deeper, into a nice, calm, totally relaxed state. So calm, so peaceful, and so, so relaxing.

"When you feel ready, imagine yourself outdoors on a beautiful sunny day. You're in a beautiful garden, and everywhere you look are flowers of indescribable beauty. The colors almost dazzle you with their brightness and intensity. You enjoy the different scents as you follow a path that takes you deeper into the garden. Bees, butterflies, and birds are all attracted to this safe haven, too, and you smile as you watch them and listen to the songs of the birds.

"You pause every now and again to look at different flowers you've never seen before and marvel at the miracles of nature. Soon you see what appears to be a central courtyard set a few steps below the rest of the garden. The courtyard is surrounded by rose bushes, all in full bloom. The path you're on appears to finish at an entrance to the courtyard, and as you walk into it, all the sounds of nature fade away, and you feel a deep sense of peace and happiness. The courtyard is made of pure white marble, and it's so beautiful you reach down and gently stroke it.

"You walk down the steps that surround the courtyard and walk over to a large pond in the center. Beautiful gold-colored fish swim lazily around the pond, and you enjoy the feeling of peace and tranquility they seem to give you.

"You notice two large chairs with cushions in your favorite color. You suddenly have an overwhelming urge to sit and relax on one of the chairs. You sink into the cushions and luxuriate in the comfort they provide. You look around, enjoying the peace, quiet, and beauty of your surroundings. You ask yourself, 'What have I done to deserve all this?'

"You suddenly hear a deep voice saying, 'You are worthy of the very best that life has to offer.' You look in the direction of the voice and see a large, good-looking man sitting in the other chair. He's smiling at you, and you can actually the feel the love emanating from him. You know that it's Archangel Michael. He's wearing white robes and sandals. His face is beautiful and exactly as you'd imagined it to be. You've been looking forward to this moment, but now that you're in Michael's presence you feel overcome.

"'Would you like me to tell you what you need to know?' Michael asks. 'Please ask me any questions you wish.'

(Allow at least three minutes of silence in the recording to enable you to ask Michael questions and listen to his answers.)

"You realize that your special time with Archangel Michael is coming to an end. You thank him for spending time with you. Michael tells you that you can call upon him whenever you wish. 'Would you do something for me?' he asks. 'When you get out of bed in the morning, I want you to look into a mirror and say, "I'm brave. I'm strong. I'm courageous. I am protected."'" Michael smiles again, and you can feel his words activating every cell of your body. 'Will you do that for me?'

"You agree, and thank him again. As you stand up, Michael fades from sight. You don't feel sad, as you know you can call on him whenever you wish. Instead of sadness, you feel full of confidence, courage, and strength. You stand for what seems a long time and then walk back up the steps and out into the beautiful garden.

"Enjoy the garden for a minute or two, and then return to your comfortable chair at home. Stretch luxuriously. Slowly count from one to five, and open your eyes."

Don't stand up immediately. Spend a minute or two thinking about your time with Archangel Michael, before getting up. Have something to eat, such as a few nuts and raisins, and drink a glass of water before carrying on with your day.

RAPHAEL
"God Heals"
Color: Green and yellow

Raphael is known as the "divine physician" because of his healing work. This isn't surprising, as the name Raphael means "God heals," and he's vitally involved in spiritual, emotional, mental, and physical healing. However, he's also involved with creativity, teaching, knowledge, science, communication, travel, and young people. He looks after the guardian angels and is considered the guardian angel of humanity.

There are many legends about Raphael's healing ability. He healed Abraham after his circumcision, for instance, and cured Jacob's dislocated hip after he'd spent a night wrestling a dark enemy at Peniel (Ginzberg, 385). In the book of Enoch, Raphael is described as being "one of the four presences, set over all the diseases and wounds of the children of men" (Enoch 1:40).

The most famous story about Raphael is told in the book of Tobit, one of the books in the Apocrypha.

Tobit was a good, honest, pious man living in the Assyrian city of Nineveh (in modern-day northern Iraq) with his wife, Anna, and son, Tobias. He was a refugee who'd worked hard and prospered. Because of his religious beliefs, he was threatened and all of his possessions were seized. During the persecution, King Sennacherib wouldn't let people bury their dead, but Tobit and a few colleagues defied this edict and secretly buried the corpses. One evening, Tobit was about to sit down for dinner when he heard of a body that needed to be buried. After doing this, he didn't return home as he'd been defiled by handling the body. Instead, he went to sleep beside a wall in his courtyard. During the night, the droppings of sparrows that were resting on the wall fell into his eyes, and when he woke up, he was totally blind.

Because he could no longer work, Anna had to earn enough money to support the family. Tobit became depressed. After eight years of blindness, he sent a prayer to heaven asking for death. At the same moment his prayer arrived in heaven, a similar one arrived from a young woman called Sarah, daughter of Raguel. An evil demon called Asmodeus had killed all seven of her husbands on their wedding night before the marriages could be consummated, and she wanted to die. God sent Raphael to answer both of these prayers.

Tobit started getting his affairs in order and asked his son Tobias to travel to Rages, a city of the Medes, to collect ten talents of silver that Gabelus, a business associate there, owed him. He asked Tobias to find someone to travel with him, as it wasn't safe for him to take the trip on his own. He offered to pay the man Tobias selected for his time and work. Tobias found a man called Azarias, who claimed to be distantly related to Tobias, to travel with him. Azarias was actually Raphael in human form, but Tobias didn't know this. They camped by the Tigris River on the first night, where a fish attacked Tobias while he was washing himself. Azarias told him to catch the fish, which Tobias did, and to cut out the fish's heart, liver, and gall. They cooked and ate the rest of the fish that evening. When Tobias asked why they saved those organs in particular, Azarias said that a smoke made from the heart and liver would exorcise evil spirits and the gall would restore the sight of a man with white film in his eyes.

When they got close to Rages, Azarias suggested they stay in the house of Raguel, and that Tobias should marry Sarah. Tobias was extremely concerned when he learned that all seven of her previous husbands had died on their wedding nights, but Azarias told him that all he had to do was to place the heart and liver on incense to create smoke. When the demon sensed the smoke, it would leave and never return.

It worked out exactly as Azarias had said. As soon as he smelled the smoke, the demon fled to "the upmost parts of Egypt" where Raphael tied him up. Everyone was delighted when Tobias and Sarah came out of the bridal chamber the next morning. Raguel, Sarah's father, was especially pleased—he'd spent the night preparing a grave for Tobias.

The wedding celebrations lasted fourteen days. Tobias collected the money that was owed to his father, and then, with Azarias and his bride, returned home to Nineveh. Tobias rubbed the gall on his father's eyes and his sight was miraculously restored. The family were overjoyed and offered Azarias half the money that Tobias had brought back with him.

Azarias then told them that he was actually Archangel Raphael, and Tobit and Tobias fell to the ground in terror. Raphael told them not to be afraid. He asked them to lead good, righteous lives, to pray to God, and to record what had happened. Tobit lived to be 158 years old. Tobias and Sarah had a long, happy marriage and were blessed with six sons. Raphael returned to heaven after fulfilling the duties of healer, guide, exorcist, and matchmaker, and is still continuing his healing ministry today.

Because of the story of Tobias and Sarah and as he's featured on the Lovers card of the Waite-Smith tarot deck, Raphael is considered a patron to Catholic singles who pray for help in finding a partner (https://www.catholicmatch.com/institute/2018/10/st-raphael-novena/ and http://www.straphael.net/saint-raphael-catholic-singles-patron.php).

Largely because of the story of Tobit, Raphael is depicted in Western art more frequently than any other angel. Rembrandt,

Raphael, Veronese, Titian, Brueghel, and Leonardo da Vinci are a few examples. Artists usually show Raphael carrying a staff, a drinking gourd, and a fish, all of which relate directly to the story of Tobit. Because of the long road trip in this story, Raphael has always been associated with travelers and enjoys helping them, especially those who are on a pilgrimage.

According to Jewish legend, Raphael taught Noah everything he needed to know to build his ark. After the flood subsided, he also gave Noah a medical book that is believed to be the *Sefer Raziel*, the book of the Angel Raziel. Raziel is thought to have given this book to Adam. At some time, the book vanished and was believed lost, until Raphael found it and presented it to Noah.

In the Testament of Solomon, Raphael also helped Solomon while he was building the Great Temple. Solomon prayed to God and asked for help with the massive project. God gave Raphael a ring with a pentagram-shaped seal on it to give to Solomon. The ring enabled Solomon to summon and order thousands of demons to work on the temple until it was finished. A pentagram has always been considered a powerful tool in magic, and many people associate Raphael with magical tools because of this story. The pentagram is also one of the earliest medical symbols, and this is again because of its association with Raphael (Conybeare, 1–45).

According to legend, Raphael was the angel who told the shepherds the glad tidings about the birth of Jesus Christ.

As Raphael's name means "God heals," it is likely that he was the angel that entered the pond named Bethesda in Jerusalem. People who were unwell waited at this pool "for the movement of water. For an angel went down at a certain season into the pool, and troubled the water: whosoever then first after the troubling of the water stepped in was made whole of whatever disease he had" (John 5:2–4).

When to Call on Archangel Raphael

You can call on Archangel Raphael whenever you need any form of healing. Raphael is willing to help you heal your spiritual, emotional, mental, and physical bodies. Naturally, you should call on Raphael whenever you are physically unwell. You can also call on Raphael when any of your loved ones are suffering from any problems with their health.

You can even ask Raphael to help heal people you don't know. Many years ago, I worked for a man who called on Archangel Raphael whenever he passed a hospital. He asked Raphael to help heal everyone inside the hospital: the patients, doctors, nurses, and everyone else involved in caring for others. When I asked him why he did this, he told me that the prayers of a stranger had helped heal his mother when she was in hospital and that he was trying to do the same.

Archangel Raphael provides additional energy for everyone who needs it. Raphael usually supplies it to people who are unwell but willingly gives it to anyone who needs extra help.

If you work in a healing profession, Raphael will provide you with guidance and additional help. Archangel Raphael will also help heal past wounds, especially emotional wounds caused by others.

If you have been through a devastating experience such as the loss of a partner or the ending of an important relationship, Archangel Raphael will help you feel complete and whole again.

Archangel Raphael Guided Visualization

You can perform a creative visualization in a matter of minutes, but it's better to set aside twenty to thirty minutes when you won't be disturbed to allow plenty of time to communicate with Archangel Raphael. Make sure that the room you're in is pleasantly warm, not too hot. Cover yourself with a rug or blanket, if the room is not as warm as you'd like. Sit down in a comfortable chair, close your eyes, and enjoy the creative visualization.

"Close your eyes, and take a nice, slow, deep breath. Allow all the muscles in your body to relax as you exhale. Take several slow, deep breaths, and allow your body to relax more and more each time you exhale. When you feel pleasantly relaxed, focus on your left foot and see if the muscles there can be relaxed even more. Once they're fully relaxed, check your calf and thigh muscles and make sure they're completely relaxed. (Pause for twenty seconds.) Do the same with your other leg. (Pause.) And now, when you're ready, allow the pleasant relaxation to drift up your body to your shoulders and neck. (Pause.) Once you've done that, check the muscles in your left arm, all the way down to the tips of your fingers. (Pause.) Do the same with your right arm. (Pause.) That's good. Finally, allow the pleasant relaxation to drift up into your face and scalp. Pay particular attention to the muscles around your eyes, and see if you can relax them more than they already are.

"In this nice, calm, pleasant, relaxed state, think of your desire to communicate with Archangel Raphael. Imagine that you're out in the countryside, walking along a path with trees and fields on either side. You've been walking for a while, but you feel invigorated and full of energy. A few small, fluffy clouds are floating in the crystal-clear sky. The only sounds are the songs of birds and an occasional moo from the cows in a nearby field.

"After a while, the path takes you through a glade where the trees provide a canopy above you. There must be a hive nearby, as you can hear the buzzing of bees, though you can't see any. The path curves slightly, and as you come near the end of the glade you can see a figure standing in the sunlight. (I see him as a tall man, dressed in casual clothes and holding a large staff. You might see him wearing robes framed by large wings. It's your visualization, and you can "see" Raphael in any form you choose.) Raphael's grinning and seems to be waiting for you. You feel a sense of excitement in every cell of your body, as you know this is the angel you've been wanting to meet, the great Archangel Raphael. As you get closer, Raphael addresses you by name and envelops you in a hug. You feel an incredible sense of peace and love inside Raphael's arms and don't want it to end.

"When he lets go, Raphael takes you by the hand and suggests you walk together for a while. You walk in comfortable silence through the fields for a minute or two. As you walk, you feel Raphael's energy revitalizing and restoring every cell in your body.

"'It's wonderful to spend quality time with you,' Raphael says. 'Please tell me what's on your mind.'

(Allow at least three minutes of silence in the recording to enable you to ask Raphael questions, and to listen to his answers.)

"Thank Raphael for always being there for you, and say you have one final request. Raphael laughs and tells you he already knows what it is. 'Let me give you a healing,' he says.

"Raphael indicates a flat rock, and you sit down on it. 'Let me hold your right hand,' Raphael says. As your hands meet, you feel a sense of peace and tranquility in every part of your body. You sense that you and Raphael are inside a bubble of pure white energy, and you're receiving spiritual, emotional, mental, and physical healing with every breath you take. You can sense every cell of your body receiving Raphael's life-giving energy and responding positively to it. You feel a brief moment of disappointment when Raphael lets go of your hand, but you also feel better than you've ever felt before. 'Thank you,' you say. 'I can't explain how wonderful I feel.'

"Raphael laughs. 'We'll do it again very soon. Call on me whenever you need more healing and energy. I'm always here for you.'

"You realize that your time with Raphael is over, but you also know that you can call on him whenever you wish. You stand up to say goodbye. 'Thank you,' you say.

"Raphael laughs again, gives you a brief hug, and then fades from view. You realize that the bubble of white light has also dissipated and you're now standing on a path out in the countryside. You sit down again, close your eyes, and think about the time you've spent with Archangel Raphael.

"When you feel ready to return to your everyday life, count slowly from one to five, and open your eyes."

Spend a minute or two thinking about the visualization, what you experienced, and how wonderful you feel now. When you get up, have something to eat and drink before carrying on with your day.

GABRIEL
"God is My Strength"
Color: White, silver, blue, light green

Gabriel is considered God's most important messenger. According to Jewish legend, Gabriel introduced herself to Abraham by saying, "I am the angel Gabriel, the messenger of God" (Ginzberg, 189). Jewish legend also tells us it was Gabriel who told Lot that the city of Sodom was going to be destroyed and that he should leave the city as quickly as he could. Gabriel also appeared to Zacharias to tell him that he and his wife Elisabeth would produce a son, whom they were to call John (Luke 1:11–17). When Zacharias queried that by telling Gabriel that he and his wife were elderly, Gabriel replied: "I am Gabriel, that stands in the presence of God; and am sent to speak unto thee, and to shew thee these glad tidings" (Luke 1:19). The son of Zacharias and Elisabeth grew up to become John the Baptist.

Gabriel is best-known to Christians as the angel who appeared before the Virgin Mary and told her that she would give birth to Jesus Christ (Luke 1:26–38). This important meeting is known as the Annunciation. Many Christians believe that Gabriel announced the birth of Jesus to the shepherds, and also warned Mary and Joseph that Herod's soldiers were searching for the newborn king.

According to Jewish legend, Gabriel and Michael served as the witnesses at Adam and Eve's wedding. Gabriel is also believed to have parted the waters of the Red Sea to enable the Israelites to escape from Pharaoh's army.

Gabriel helps earthly messengers, such as writers and teachers. In 1951, Pope Pius XII declared Archangel Gabriel the patron saint of postal workers, which means that God's main messenger looks after the people who deliver messages. In addition to these duties as God's most important messenger, Gabriel helps people overcome doubts and fears, and provides help, guidance, and advice in the form of dreams and visions. Gabriel's other tasks are to help people with problems and concerns relating to conception, pregnancy, birth, and a child's early years. Examples of these are when she acted as a guardian angel for both Abraham and Moses when they were infants.

Gabriel is also considered the angel of dreams, premonitions, and clairvoyance. This is because Gabriel helped Daniel understand the meanings of his strange dreams (Daniel 8:16–27). Daniel had dreamed of a ram with two horns, which was defeated by a goat with one horn. Gabriel told him that the ram symbolized the empire of the Medes and the Persians. The goat symbolized the king of the Greeks who would come and destroy them. The dream came true almost two hundred years later when Alexander and his army took over most of the known world. On another occasion, Gabriel told Daniel about the coming Messiah and the destruction of Jerusalem (Daniel 9:21–27).

The Harmonists, a nineteenth-century Christian sect, claimed that Gabriel had appeared to their leader, Father George Rapp (1757–1847) in New Harmony, Indiana, and had left her footprint on a limestone slab that can still be seen in the yard of the Maclure-Owen residence (Fretageot and Mangrum, 29–30).

Gabriel as Jibril (the Islamic name for Gabriel) appeared to the prophet Muhammad and dictated the Koran to him. Gabriel appeared in the shape of different people, but on one occasion Muhammad asked if he could see Gabriel as he actually was. Gabriel appeared in male form with his wings outstretched, and his shape filled the entire sky. Muhammad also saw Gabriel as a cloud and, on another occasion, Gabriel demonstrated his power by beating six hundred wings (Ali, 178).

An old Babylonian legend tells how Gabriel was demoted for twenty-one days from her position in charge of the sixth heaven to be replaced by Dubbiel, the guardian angel of the Persians. Apparently, Jehovah was angry with the Jewish people for some reason and asked Gabriel to destroy them. She was told to pour burning coals on top of them and then allow the Babylonians to kill the survivors.

Gabriel felt sorry for the Israelites and so asked the laziest angel in heaven to help her. This angel took so long to pass the coals to Gabriel that they had cooled down by the time Gabriel threw them to earth. Gabriel then persuaded the Babylonians not to kill the Jews and suggested they force the Jews into Babylon instead.

Disappointed with Gabriel's actions, Jehovah replaced her with Dubbiel. With Dubbiel's help, the Persians cruelly oppressed the Jewish people. Fortunately, Gabriel gave God a different good suggestion, and after a few weeks she was reinstated to her former position. Dubbiel eventually became one of the fallen angels (Bunson, 81, 115).

One of my favorite stories about Gabriel tells how she teaches unborn babies about their mission in their upcoming lifetimes and then swears the babies to keep this knowledge secret. The promise is made as Gabriel presses her finger on the babies' lips, creating the philtrum, the indentation under the nose.

When to Call on Archangel Gabriel

You can call on Archangel Gabriel whenever you need purification, inspiration, or help in finding your true calling in life. Gabriel is also willing to help you if you feel vulnerable after any form of attack—mental or physical assault, theft, psychic attack, and sexual assault. Archangel Gabriel will provide the necessary cleansing and purification you'll need after experiencing any horrific incident.

Gabriel will also help whenever you feel negative, unmotivated, or overwhelmed with problems. She also helps you resolve fears, doubts, and worries. This archangel will help if you're wanting to develop your intuitive and spiritual potential—you can ask that you receive information in the form of dreams, visions, or prophecies.

Gabriel will help you develop your creative abilities by providing inspiration, encouragement, and guidance; she also enjoys helping people find their true path in this lifetime. If necessary, ask Gabriel to help you understand your soul's purpose and to provide guidance as to how to achieve it. Gabriel will also provide guidance whenever you're thinking about making an important change such as a change in career, moving to a new home, or starting a family.

Archangel Gabriel Guided Visualization

A guided visualization is a highly effective way to communicate with Archangel Gabriel whenever you're suffering from doubts and fears, and need guidance, inspiration, encouragement, and purification. All you need is twenty to thirty minutes of uninterrupted time in a warm and comfortable location.

Close your eyes, relax your body, and allow yourself to follow the words in the guided visualization. You can record these words, if you wish, and play them back to yourself. Alternatively, you could read the script several times, to get the general idea of it, and then relax and say it to yourself using your own words. There are advantages and disadvantages to both methods. Listening to a recorded script is easy, as once you're relaxed, all you need do is listen to the words and imagine and visualize each stage of the process. However, a recorded script forces you to move at a particular pace. You can speak to Archangel Gabriel for a maximum of three minutes, for example. It also might take longer for you to relax completely than the recording allows. Saying the script to yourself is harder to do, as you need to keep your mind focused on your intention. However, it does allow you to spend as long as necessary to relax, and you can speak with Gabriel for as long as you wish. If you haven't done any creative visualization in the past, it would pay to record and listen to the script a number of times before trying the other method.

Here is the script for the Archangel Gabriel's Creative Visualization:

"Make yourself comfortable, close your eyes, and allow your body to relax. It's so quiet and peaceful, and you're drifting deeper and deeper into pleasant relaxation with every breath you take. Soon you'll notice that your breathing has become slower and deeper, as you become more and more relaxed. Nothing need bother or disturb you as you drift deeper into pleasant relaxation.

"This is your own special time, and you can let go of all the problems and hassles of everyday life. You're about to spend some quality time with Archangel Gabriel, and to do that you need to be peaceful, calm, and relaxed.

"In this nice, calm, peaceful state, focus on your feet and toes. Sense if they hold any tension and then let those muscles dissolve as you allow them to relax. Now think of the muscles in your calves and knees and let them relax too. It's so pleasant to feel the muscles relax completely and totally. Move your attention to the large muscles in your thighs and allow them to let go of any tension or tightness they might be holding. Allow the pleasant relaxation to drift into your buttocks and pelvis, gradually moving up to your stomach and lower back. When they feel totally relaxed, allow the relaxation to drift into your back and chest. Feel the relaxation moving into your shoulders and down each arm to the tips of your fingers.

"You're almost totally relaxed now. Sense the relaxation moving into your neck and face, all the way up to the top of your head. Now let the fine muscles around your eyes relax.

"Mentally scan your body to make sure that you are completely relaxed. If necessary, focus on any areas that still hold some tension and feel them dissolve as they let go.

"And now, imagine yourself floating through time and space, feeling totally free to go anywhere you wish. You're searching for the perfect place to meet Archangel Gabriel. In your imagination, choose the most beautiful and peaceful place you can imagine. It might be a place that you've visited many times in reality, it could be a place that you've always wanted to visit, or maybe it's a place you've created in your mind. You might even choose to go backward or forward in time. It doesn't matter where you go, just as long as you feel comfortable and safe inside the scene.

"Once you've found the perfect place for your meeting with Gabriel, find somewhere to sit and relax. Look around and enjoy the magnificent colors and the beauty that surrounds you. When you feel ready, silently ask Archangel Gabriel to join you. You may have to wait a minute or two, but you know in your heart that Gabriel will come to see you.

"You'll suddenly realize that Gabriel has arrived and is standing directly in front of you. (Gabriel will appear in whatever form you imagine. In the Bible, Gabriel is believed to appear in the form of a male, but because of Gabriel's interest in nurturing and other traditionally feminine activities, many people see Gabriel as a female. Gabriel may or may not have wings—it's entirely up to you.)

"Gabriel starts by giving you a blessing, and then sits down beside you. 'Tell me, what's going in your life?' Gabriel asks. You tell Gabriel about your past, present, and hopes for the future. You then ask as many specific questions as you wish."

(Allow at least three minutes of silence in the recording to enable you to ask Gabriel questions and listen to the answers. If you have a specific goal you need help with, use this time to ask Gabriel for help, advice, and encouragement.)

"Thank Gabriel for being so helpful, nurturing, understanding, and for always being there for you. Gabriel stands up, and you do too. Gabriel embraces you, and you feel a surge of love and joy in every cell of your body. Gabriel holds the hug for several seconds, and you have just enough time to say goodbye before Gabriel disappears.

"You sit down again and think about the amazing experience you've just had. You feel so happy that you'll be able to repeat it whenever you wish. When you feel ready, feel yourself floating through time and space again until you're back where you started. Wait a minute or two before counting from one to five and opening your eyes."

Spend a minute or two thinking about the visualization, what you experienced, and how happy you feel now. When you get up, have something to eat and drink before carrying on with your day.

URIEL
"Fire of God"
Color: Red, yellow, orange, and blue

Uriel provides clarity, insight, and inner peace. He interprets prophecies and brings knowledge of God to humankind. Uriel enjoys helping people engaged in creative work. He also helps people progress materially while at the same time remaining aware of the Divine. He's in charge of natural phenomena, such as floods and earthquakes (Enoch 20:2). In Jewish legend, it was Uriel who warned Noah of the imminent flood (Enoch 1:1–3). The Sibylline Oracles state that Uriel also looks after the keys to hell and will destroy the gates to hell on Judgment Day. Uriel punishes sinners when they deserve it but is more than willing to help people who need it. In the apocryphal book of Adam and Eve, Uriel is the angel of repentance. Uriel also encourages dreams, visions, and prophecies.

As the archangel of prophecy, Uriel is often depicted with a book or scroll in one hand and a burning flame on the palm of his other hand. Uriel is usually listed as one of the four main archangels. However, unlike Michael, Gabriel, and Raphael, he doesn't appear in the canonical scriptures, which means we know him only through stories and legends. He's identified by name in the book of Esdras: "The angel that was sent unto me, whose name was Uriel, gave me an answer" (Book 2:4).

Uriel is a gifted teacher and was Enoch's guide and teacher during most of his tour of the heavens. Uriel taught astronomy, time, and Hebrew characters to Seth, Adam's son (Joel, 3). Uriel also arranged for Ezra to have seven prophetic dreams to help explain that evil has a certain amount of time to run its course. Uriel helped Ezra interpret and understand the messages in his dreams (Ginzberg, 356–357).

According to the Apocalypse of Moses, Uriel and Michael were the angels who buried Adam in heaven. However, a number of texts discuss Adam's burial; the numbers of angels who were present varies considerably (Ginzberg, 125).

A Hebrew legend tells that after Cain killed Abel, he tried to bury him but the earth kept bringing the body back up to the surface. Uriel, Michael, Gabriel, and Raphael witnessed this and after Cain fled, they put the body on a rock, where it lay for many years without decomposing.

Although his name is not mentioned in the Bible, Uriel is believed to be the angel of the Lord who destroyed the hosts of Sennacherib (II Kings 19:35). Many sources say he was the angel who wrestled with Jacob for a full night. Michael, Samael, and Phanuel have all been suggested as the angels who wrestled with Jacob. Phanuel is the one who is mentioned most frequently because the name Phanuel is similar to Peniel, the name of the place where the wrestling occurred. Phanuel is often thought to be another name for Uriel. However, the book of Enoch clearly states that they are two different angels.

In the apocryphal book of Esdras, Esdras reproached God for helping Israel's enemies. Uriel, who was travelling with Esdras, replied that he'd reveal God's reasons after the prophet had weighed fire, measured the wind, and brought back the previous day. Esdras said that he could do none of those things. Uriel said that if Esdras knew the fire, wind, and days, but could not understand them, how could he possibly understand God's intentions when he did not know Him? Esdras immediately fell at Uriel's feet and asked for forgiveness.

A number of early Christian writings say that Uriel is also supposed to have been the angel who rescued the infant John the Baptist and his mother, Elisabeth, when King Herod ordered the slaughter of innocent children. Uriel carried them to Egypt to join Jesus and his family. Leonardo da Vinci recorded the moment the two families were reunited in his painting, *Virgin of the Rocks*.

Francis Barrett, the nineteenth-century occultist, wrote that Uriel brought the great gift of alchemy to humankind (Barrett, 57). Starting in 1582, Dr. John Dee (1527–1608), mathematician, philosopher, astronomer, and Queen Elizabeth the First's astrologer, worked closely with Uriel from his home in Mortlake, near London, with the help of his assistant, Edward Kelley, who was a gifted scryer. Kelley contacted Uriel on their first scrying session. This was exciting, as Dee had read that Uriel taught astrology to Enoch the prophet. Dee and Edward Kelley began communicating with Uriel, Gabriel, Raphael, Michael, and other angels on a regular basis. In March 1583, Kelley had a vision of a book that had to be filled with the angelic language (known today as the Enochian language). Dee and Kelley were told that this language was the same one that God had taught to Enoch thousands of years before. The language they laboriously produced, one letter at a time, and writing from right to left, is remarkable: it contains its own script, grammar, and syntax and doesn't appear to be closely related to any other language. The work was completed on July 13, 1584, and shortly after that, Uriel and the other angels stopped communicating their systems of angelic magic to them.

All this work was done by scrying, but John Dee possibly saw Uriel on two occasions. The first occasion happened in 1582, the year he met Edward Kelley, when he had a vision of a child angel, holding a crystal egg, floating outside his window. John Dee recognized this angel as Uriel (Heline, 110). On another occasion, Edward Kelley saw a cherub in a crystal ball, which Dee was able to identify as "Uriel, the Angel of Light."

John Dee and Edward Kelley recorded a huge amount of information but weren't interested in using it themselves. Three centuries later, S. L. MacGregor Mathers (1854–1918), one of the founders of the Hermetic Order of the Golden Dawn, recognized its worth and included parts of Enochian magic in the Golden Dawn teachings. Today, there is more interest in Dr. John Dee and the Enochian language than ever before. It's fortunate that this gifted man, who was almost lost to history, is recognized and appreciated much more today than he was in his lifetime.

An ancient Jewish legend says that Uriel gave the Kabbalah to humankind. In the Kabbalah, Uriel is associated with the middle pillar of the Tree of Life and with Malkuth, the sephira that represents the world we live in. Sandalphon is the archangel of Malkuth, and he and Uriel work together to ensure the health and survival of planet Earth.

Uriel is archangel of the earth and consequently is responsible for everything that Mother Nature does, from the ripening of the crops to tidal waves and earthquakes. Many people, myself included, say, "Hello, Uriel," when they see a rainbow appear after a storm. As part of his work as archangel of the earth, Uriel looks after nature spirits and fairies. Uriel acts as a channel between the Earth and the Divine. He brings peace and tranquility to people who need it. He releases pain and trauma from the past and helps people start moving forward again. He provides the gifts of prophecy, creativity, and divine light.

Uriel has many titles, including Angel of the Eleventh Hour, Angel of Repentance, Angel of Prophecy, Prince of the Sun, Angel of Thunder and Lightning, Angel of Salvation, and Angel of Terror. This last title shows that Uriel, like the other archangels, is prepared to use his power when necessary. In addition, Uriel has been known by a number of names, including Ariel, Auriel, Hamiel, Hanael, and Phanael. Auriel means "Light of God," Hamiel means "Grace of God," and Hanael means the "Face of God."

As Auriel, the archangel of light, Uriel can help you receive the divine light that mystics receive when they experience sudden insights that make them as one with the Divine. William G. Gray (1913–1992), the British ceremonial magician and author, wrote: "A single flash from Auriel will put us closer to God in an instant than centuries of our muddling speculations" (Gray, 88).

When to Call on Archangel Uriel

You can call on Archangel Uriel whenever you want to banish fear and gain inner peace. You can ask Uriel to bring peace to individuals, countries, and the world.

Archangel Uriel enjoys helping people develop their prophetic gifts, such as the tarot or dream interpretation.

Uriel provides clarity, insight, and vision, enabling you to understand other people's motives and possibly hidden agendas.

Archangel Uriel Guided Visualization

A guided visualization is a convenient way to contact Archangel Uriel when you're feeling overwhelmed with problems and need a new perspective on life. You can also call upon him for inner peace, insight, psychic development, and abundance.

Record the following script ahead of time to allow it to help you relax. If you have a partner or friend with similar interests, they could read the script to you and you could reciprocate in turn. Alternatively, you could make yourself familiar with the script and be able to silently say it to yourself while you relax and enjoy the visualization.

Sit or lie down somewhere where you won't be interrupted for twenty to thirty minutes. Make yourself comfortable and allow your body to relax.

Here is the script for the Archangel Uriel Guided Visualization:

"Take a nice, slow, deep breath, and close your eyes as you exhale. Inhale again, and silently say the word 'relax' to yourself as you exhale. Continue breathing this way until your breathing has slowed down and you're feeling pleasantly relaxed. Make a fist with your right hand and squeeze it tight. Now relax your right hand as much as you can. Notice how different the feeling is between tense and relaxed muscles.

"Mentally scan your body and deliberately relax any areas of tension. Relax the muscles in your feet and then relax the muscles all the way up your legs to your thighs. Feel the tension fading away as you do this. (Pause.) Allow the relaxation to move into your abdomen and stomach muscles, and to then drift into your chest and back. (Pause.) If any areas seem unwilling to relax, clench the muscles and then let go. Feel the tension fade and disappear when you do this.

"Focus on your shoulder muscles now, and after relaxing them, allow the relaxation to drift down your arms and hands. (Pause.) When they're fully relaxed, allow the muscles in your neck to relax, and then move up to your head, relaxing your forehead, jaw, and the fine muscles around your eyes. Relax the muscles in your scalp, and then take another slow, deep breath.

"In this nice, calm, relaxed state, you're ready to meet Archangel Uriel. In your imagination, look up into the clear blue sky. It's a beautiful, sunny day, and you can see only one cloud in the sky. It's a fluffy white cloud, and you enjoy watching its movements as it floats first one way, and then another, almost as if it was playing in a sea of blue. As you watch, it seems to come a little bit closer to you, and then a little bit more. After a few moments, you realize that it's getting lower and lower, and soon you're completely enveloped by this beautiful cloud. The cloud fills you with a deep sense of peace and tranquility. You feel safe, secure, and so, so relaxed.

"The cloud starts moving upwards again, carrying you with it. You feel a sense of excitement and anticipation, as you know the cloud is taking you to see Archangel Uriel. Your whole body is tingling with positivity and happiness.

"The cloud stops moving, and you hear a clear voice calling you by name. You can't see him yet, but you know this must be Archangel Uriel. Suddenly, he's beside you and you feel emotion in your heart and throat. You want to speak but your throat chakra is blocked with emotion. You gaze up at Uriel and see love, tenderness, and compassion in this great archangel's smiling face. You smile back and discover you've regained the ability to speak. 'Thank you for seeing me,' you say.

"Uriel puts an arm around you, and you feel your body absorbing his pure, healthy, peaceful energy. 'The pleasure is all mine,' Uriel replies. 'How may I help you?'

(Allow at least three minutes of silence in the recording to enable you to ask Uriel questions and listen to the answers.)

"When you've finished asking questions, thank Archangel Uriel for all his help and support. Uriel puts his arm around you again and turns it into a hug. You feel incredibly blessed and happy that this great archangel is willing to give his valuable time to help you. You thank him again and ask if you could contact him again soon. "'I'm always ready to help,'" Uriel replies. He smiles again and then quickly fades from view.

"You lie comfortably inside the fluffy white cloud, feeling safe, protected, and in total control of your life. You have a clear idea of what you want to do and how to achieve it. You feel excited and happy that you can contact Uriel whenever you need his advice or counsel.

"You notice that you can control the movements of the cloud with your thoughts. After making it move from side to side and up and down, you direct it back down to the ground. It takes only a few moments, and you find yourself back where you started. The cloud rises upwards again, leaving you behind. You gaze up at the clear blue sky and the one fluffy cloud and send a final, sincere thank-you to Archangel Uriel. Wait for a minute or two, then count slowly from one to five and open your eyes."

Many people feel slightly spaced-out after a visualization of this sort. Consequently, make sure to ground yourself by eating a few nuts and raisins, and having something to drink, before carrying on with your day.

Raphael, Michael, Gabriel, and Uriel feature in every list of archangels. However, many other angels have also been called "archangels." We'll look at the most important of these in the next chapter.

THE LESSER-KNOWN ARCHANGELS

Many angels have been considered archangels, and it's impossible to include all of them here. For instance, in the second book of Esdras, written in the second century CE, there's a list of the nine angels who will be in charge at the end of the world. Michael, Gabriel, Raphael, and Uriel are listed, followed by Gabuthelon, Aker, Arphugitonos, Beburos, and Zebuleon. The first four are archangels, but as the other five aren't mentioned anywhere else, no one knows what positions these angels hold. As the angels themselves aren't interested in the human concept of hierarchies, it's impossible to know exactly which ones are archangels, and which ones aren't. The angels in this chapter have all been considered archangels by a number of authorities, and, even if they don't all belong in the choir of archangels, they deserve your attention, as you can call upon them for help and advice whenever you need it.

ADNACHIEL
"The Shining One"
Color: White, blue

Adnachiel, the angel of independence, helps people who are interested in adventure and excitement. He looks after Sagittarians and the month of November. He provides optimism, hope, humility, and confidence and helps people overcome fears, doubts, and worries. Adnachiel is an angel of truth; he helps people recognize it when they find it. He wants people to be honest and ethical in all their dealings. Adnachiel fills people with a desire to learn and grow in knowledge and wisdom. He also helps people find their purpose in this lifetime. Adnachiel and Phaleg are said to be the angels governing the choir of angels in heaven.

AMBRIEL
"The Energy of God"
Color: Purple, red, pink

Ambriel (also known as Amriel) is prince of the choir of thrones, and is the archangel who looks after the month of May, and the astrological sign of Gemini. When Ambriel appears, she usually has long, blonde hair, and wears a rose-red jacket. She also has a silver belt.

As Ambriel wards off evil, she is usually depicted with one hand raised in front of her to repel all forms of negativity. Ambriel helps people to think clearly and can also be contacted for any matters involving communication. She is also willing to help people who are looking for new jobs or are seeking more opportunities and responsibilities.

ANAEL
"The Grace of God"
Color: Dark green, blue

Anael (also known as Aniel or Haniel) is said to be one of the seven archangels of creation but is not listed as an archangel by Pseudo-

Dionysius or Saint Gregory. However, both Thomas Heywood, author of *The Hierarchy of Blessed Angels* (1635), and Rudolf Steiner (1861–1925), philosopher, author, and founder of Anthroposophy, named Anael as one of the seven great archangels. He is generally considered a prince of the choirs of principalities and virtues and is usually depicted by artists wearing a crown to signify his status and importance.

Anael rules the month of December, and looks after people born under the sign of Capricorn. He is also one of the planetary angels and is associated with Venus. Because of this, Anael is closely linked to affection and love and is possibly the most-invoked angel of all. He can be called upon for any matter involving affection, love, romance, sexuality, peace, harmony, and peace of mind. He enjoys helping people who suffer from shyness and lack of confidence. He also helps people interested in progressing in their careers, gaining status, and receiving recognition for their accomplishments. In addition to this, Anael also helps people involved in creative activities and tries to create beauty everywhere he goes. Anael is governor of the second heaven and attends to all the prayers rising from the first heaven.

An intriguing verse in the Bible appears to say that Enoch, after living for three hundred and sixty-five years, didn't die but was instead taken directly to heaven: "And Enoch walked with God: and he was not; for God took him" (Genesis 5:24). According to the book of Enoch, it was Anael who transported Enoch to heaven in a fiery chariot drawn by fiery horses (3 Enoch 6:1–18).

Anael is also said to be the angel who called out: "Open ye the gates, that the righteous nation which keepeth the truth may enter in" (Isaiah 26:2).

ARIEL
"Lion of God"
Color: Yellow, pink

Ariel (also known as Ariel and Ariael) is one of the seventy-two Schemhamphoras, a group of angels who bear the various names of God found in Jewish scriptures. He is mentioned in the pseudepigraphic Book of Ezra and *The Key of Solomon the King*. The English poet and playwright Thomas Heywood (ca. 1574–1641) called him "Earth's greatest Lord" in his *Hierarchy of the Blessed Angels* (1635). He is also one of the ruling angels of the zodiac and is responsible for the sign of Leo.

Ariel helps people set goals and achieve them. He also helps them find and develop hidden talents and skills. Ariel helps people find the inner strength, courage, and persistence they need to achieve their goals. Ariel has a strong interest in the natural world, too, and is willing to help people who are involved in the care and welfare of animals and plants. Ariel calls on Raphael for assistance whenever necessary to heal animals, plants, and the environment. Ariel helps people see the beauty in nature everywhere they go. As Ariel is an angel of abundance, he is always willing to help people manifest whatever it is they desire.

ASARIEL
"Whom God Has Bound"
Color: Sea green

Asariel is one of the planetary angels and ruler of the planet Neptune. Asariel is one of the twenty-eight angels who look after the twenty-eight mansions of the moon.

Asariel encourages people who are interested in developing their intuition and helps people involved in clairvoyance and mediumship. She also helps people develop their creative imaginations. Traditionally, Asariel can be called upon to help heal sick horses.

ASMODEL
"I Become"
Color: Green

Asmodel (also known as Asmodiel) governs the month of April and the sign of Taurus. He was formerly one of the rulers of the choir of cherubim. Asmodel is cautious and advises slow, steady progress as the best way to increase net worth. He is patient and likes to slowly and carefully assess any situation before acting. He remains calm and relaxed, even in difficult situations. He helps people recognize the spiritual side of their natures and encourages them to develop this aspect of their being. Asmodel can be called upon for any matter involving love, romance, and close relationships.

AZRAEL
"Whom God Helps"
Color: Yellow, cream

Azrael (also known as Azrail, Azriel, and Azaril) lives in the third heaven and is considered the angel of death in the Hebrew and Islamic traditions. Azrael records everybody's names when they're born and erases them when they die. His main task is to escort people to the afterlife once their lifetime has come to an end. He comforts people as they're dying, and makes sure their journey to the other side is as comfortable and painless as possible. He remains with them long enough to help them become used to their new lives. Azrael also provides help and solace for grieving relatives who are mourning their loss. An important part of his work is to help people communicate with their deceased loved ones. He's a useful angel to call upon if you're working on a family history or are creating a family tree. Azrael is one of the planetary angels and is considered ruler of Pluto.

In Jewish and Islamic lore, Azrael is known as Israfil and is considered the angel of death. This is because when God decided to create Adam, he sent Michael, Gabriel, and Israfil to earth to collect seven handfuls of dirt that God would use to create the first man. The earth refused this request, as it believed mankind would create nothing but pain and suffering. The three angels had to return to heaven and tell God that they'd failed. God then sent Azrael down to earth. He forcibly obtained the necessary dirt and brought it back to heaven. As a reward for doing this, God decreed that Azrael would be responsible for releasing the human soul from the physical body at the moment of death.

Although Israfil is the fourth archangel in Islam, he has no idea when someone is going to die. Allah writes the person's name on a leaf and drops it from his throne. Israfil picks it up and collects the person's soul forty days later.

Israfil is a huge angel. He is so large that if all the water in the world was poured on his head, none of it would reach the ground. He has four thousand wings and four faces that are covered by a million veils. He has as many eyes and tongues as there are people living on earth. Every time Israfil blinks, it means that someone has died.

Azrael can be called upon when exploring past lifetimes, and is willing to help anyone who is seriously interested in exploring the psychic world. Azrael also provides strength, comfort, and healing energy to people who are grieving, and suffering from emotional or mental health problems. Azrael helps people who are struggling to overcome addictions, depression, and feelings of unworthiness.

BARBIEL
"Illumination of God"
Color: Green

Barbiel (also known as Barbuel and Baruel) is responsible for the month of October and looks after the interests of people born under the zodiac sign of Scorpio. He's a prince of both the choir of archangels and the choir of virtues. He is also one of the twenty-eight angels who govern the mansions of the moon. He has a keen interest in astrology.

There seem to be two angels called Barbiel. The other one is a fallen angel who is one of the seven electors of hell.

BARCHIEL
"God's Blessings"
Color: Green

Barchiel (also known as Barakiel, Barachiel, Barkiel, and Baraqiel) is one of the eighteen rulers of earth and, according to the third book of Enoch, has 496,000 angels ministering to him. Barchiel is ruler of the order of seraphim, prince of the second heaven, and a leading member of the sarim, the 550 ruling angels King Solomon worked with. Today they spend their time singing the praises of the Lord. In the Eastern Orthodox tradition, Barchiel is considered one of the seven archangels and chief of the guardian angels. He looks after the month of February and the astrological sign of Pisces. Different texts suggest that Barchiel fulfills a variety of roles.

As the aAngel of blessings, Barchiel is often depicted scattering rose petals that represent God's blessings to the world. Usually, some of the petals are on his cloak as well as on the ground. Barchiel frequently asks God to provide blessings to people who need them.

Barchiel helps people increase their confidence and develop a positive outlook on life. Because he provides abundance and good fortune, gamblers will often invoke him, usually calling him Barakiel. He provides happiness and stability to home and family life, and can be called upon to help when families find themselves in difficult situations. He also encourages people to use humor to help them handle the inevitable ups and downs of life.

CAMAEL
"He Who Sees God"
Color: Rose red

Camael (also known as Camniel, Kemuel, Kameel, and Qemuel) is ruler of the choir of powers. He also rules the planet Mars, sharing this role with Samael. He is said to be one of the seven angels who stand in the presence of God. There are legends that say he was the angel who wrestled with Jacob and that he appeared to Jesus in the Garden of Gethsemane. However, Paniel is more usually considered the angel who wrestled with Jacob, and Gabriel is almost always thought to be the angel who visited Jesus.

Camael provides courage, energy, and strength to people who desperately need it.

CAMBIEL
"I empower"
Color: Lavender, blue

Cambiel is one of the angels of the zodiac and looks after people born under the sign of Aquarius. He also looks after the month of January. He's interested in science, technology, and the future. Anything else that's new and progressive appeals to him.

Cambiel is the angel of transformation and can turn situations around at the speed of lightning. With Cambiel's help, the impossible can become not only possible but a reality. Consequently, Cambiel is an archangel of manifestation. Cambiel also encourages original thinking and helps people involved in study and learning.

CASSIEL
"Speed of God"
Color: Emerald green, dark brown

Cassiel (also known as Casiel and Kafziel) is a ruling prince of the seventh heaven and one of the princes of the choir of powers. He's also one of the rulers of Saturn and the astrological sign of Capricorn. As Saturn is a slow-moving planet that takes four years to orbit the sun, it can sometimes take Cassiel a long time to resolve a problem. Fortunately, Archangel Raphael is happy to encourage Cassiel to speed up the process.

As Lord of the seventh heaven (which is where God lives), Cassiel has the important task of determining who can enter into this holy of holies. Cassiel works with both royalty and people who are struggling to survive. At these two extremes, he is present at the deaths of kings and also helps the downtrodden, the oppressed, the wrongly persecuted, and children living in poverty.

Cassiel is usually depicted by artists as an angry-looking man with a dark beard. He wears a crown to show that he is the prince in charge of the seventh heaven. He holds an arrow made from a feather and rides a dragon.

Cassiel helps people learn patience. He helps them do whatever is necessary to resolve their problems and gives them serenity and peace of mind. Cassiel is the angel of karma. He helps people understand the law of cause and effect and teaches moderation, temperance, stability, and serenity.

CHAMUEL

"He Who Seeks God"
Color: Pink, orange, light green

Chamuel (also known as Camuel, Camiel, Jahoel, Khamael, Semibel, and Simiel) is one of the seven archangels and a prince of the choir of dominions. He's in charge of maintaining peace in the world and is therefore known as the archangel of peace. He can be called upon to help resolve disputes and legal problems of any scale. He is just as happy helping people resolve their career or relationship difficulties as he is in working to establish world peace. Chamuel is also the archangel of peace, compassion, and unconditional love. Some sources say that it was Chamuel who comforted Jesus in the Garden of Gethsemane. However, the Bible does not identify this angel by name; it is usually thought to be Gabriel. In the Kabbalah, Chamuel (spelled Khamael) is considered one of the seven great archangels and represents Geburah (strength) in the Tree of Life.

Chamuel is the archangel of unconditional love. He encourages harmonious relationships, soothes troubled minds, rights wrongs, and provides justice. He helps people to forgive others, especially people who were or are close to them. He helps people who have gone through relationship breakups, gives them hope for the future, and is willing to help them find true love. He helps people express their deepest feelings through some form of creativity. He helps people make the right career choices, and then progress in their chosen field. Chamuel also provides tolerance, strength, courage, determination, and persistence.

HAMALIEL
"Grace of God"
Color: Brown, yellow, red

Hamaliel is chief of the choir of virtues and the archangel who looks after the month of August and the zodiac sign of Virgo.

Hamaliel is the angel of harvest and abundance in every sense of the word. She helps people think logically and clearly and retain what they have learned. Hamaliel can be invoked for anything that involves logic, care, self-discipline, patience, and attention to detail. She enjoys working with students, teachers, and anyone else involved in education, including self-education. Hamaliel is also in charge of all the chemical processes on earth; in this role, she looks after chemists and other people studying or working in the sciences.

HANAEL
"Glory of God"
Color: Light blue, turquoise, green

Hanael (also known as Anaphiel, Aniel, Hamiel, Hanael, and Onoel) is considered one of the ten main archangels. Ruler of the planet Venus, she is also one of the rulers of the choirs of principalities and virtues. She's also the angel who looks after December and the astrological sign of Capricorn. In his book, *The Magus*, Francis Barrett wrote that Hanael was ruler of the choir of innocents. Thomas Heywood wrote that Hanael was one of the seven great archangels in his 1635 book, *The Hierarchy of Blessed Angels*.

There's an intriguing verse in the Bible that intimates that Enoch didn't die but was transported to heaven: "And Enoch walked with God: and he was not; for God took him" (Genesis 5:24). Enoch 3 says that Hanael was the angel who transported Enoch to heaven in a fiery chariot (3 Enoch 6:1–18). In this story in the book of Enoch, Hanael is known as Anaphiel. Hanael is also a planetary angel, and she has a strong interest in natural healing and the psychic world.

Although angels are genderless and can appear in any form they wish, Hanael is usually depicted as a female angel, and is associated with compassion, love, harmony, balance, beauty, and refinement. She helps people to value themselves, realize their skills and potentials, and make significant progress in this incarnation. She has a particular interest in healing family relationships, and enjoys helping people start to communicate with each other again. She also enjoys helping people discover their spiritual and intuitive abilities. Hanael has a powerful, yet gentle, energy that helps people become aware of their purpose in this incarnation.

JEHUDIEL
"Praise of God"
Color: Purple

Jehudiel is one of the seven archangels in the Eastern Orthodox Church. He is usually depicted holding a crown in one hand and a three-tailed whip in the other. These indicate God's reward for the righteous and punishment for the sinners.

Jehudiel provides opportunities and encouragement to people who are honest, sincere, and prepared to work hard to achieve worthwhile spiritual goals. He also helps people who are looking for work or want to progress in their careers. He has a special interest in helping people build up their confidence and self-esteem.

JEREMIEL
"Mercy of God"
Color: Purple

Jeremiel is an angel of transition who encourages people to make positive changes in their lives. She brings matters that have been kept secret or hidden out into the open. She is sometimes thought to be one of the gatekeepers of heaven, and helps escort people's souls as they start their afterlife journey. Jeremiel is also an angel of mercy and forgiveness who helps people to forgive others as well as themselves. Jeremiel usually communicates in the form of visions and dreams, and encourages people who are interested in developing their psychic and spiritual abilities.

In 2 Esdras 4:36, Jeremiel is said to be an archangel. Although Jeremiel is also mentioned in the book of Esdras (4:36–37) and the first book of Enoch, it's possible that her name is another name for Ramiel, Remiel, or Uriel.

In 2 Baruch, which is part of the Jewish and Christian Apocrypha, Jeremiel is said to be the angel who "presides over true visions" (2 Baruch 55:3). This is because Baruch experienced a vision of dark water and bright water that Archangel Jeremiel interpreted. She told Baruch that the dark water illustrates how human sin causes great devastation in the world, and the bright water shows how a caring God intervenes to help humanity (2 Baruch 71:1–3). Jeremiel also gave Baruch hope for the future by showing him a vision of what the world will be like without pain, suffering, anger, hatred, and revenge (2 Baruch 73:1–4). After this, Jeremiel took Baruch on a tour of the heavens.

Jeremiel helps people make good career choices, and encourages them to create the very best life that they can. She works with people to help them overcome difficult and painful situations, and learn valuable lessons from these experiences. She also helps people to understand and interpret their dreams.

JOPHIEL
"Beauty of God"
Color: Gold, yellow, pink

Jophiel (also known as Iofiel, Iophiel, and Zophiel) is one of the rulers of the choir of cherubim. (However, some sources say that he's actually ruler of the order of thrones.) Pseudo-Dionysius included him in his list of seven archangels. According to German mystic and alchemist Heinrich Cornelius Agrippa (1486–1535), Jophiel is the ruler of the planet Saturn, alternating in this role with Zaphkiel (Agrippa, 468).

According to legend, Jophiel guarded the Tree of Knowledge in the Garden of Eden. Jophiel is also thought to be the angel who expelled Adam and Eve from the Garden of Eden and who taught and guided Noah's three sons, Shem, Ham, and Japheth.

Jophiel provides joy and laughter everywhere he goes. He loves beauty and can be called upon to help with all kinds of creative endeavors. Jophiel encourages people to slow down and appreciate all the beauty that surrounds them. Jophiel beautifies everything he is associated with and can even beautify people's minds by turning negative thoughts into positive ones. Even in difficult times, Jophiel helps people see the beauty in all things. Not surprisingly, he's considered the patron angel of artists. Jophiel is usually depicted wielding a flaming sword of wisdom, the idea being that the sword provides clarity and enables people to clearly understand their thoughts, feelings, and emotions. It cuts through illusions and self-deception to reveal the truth. Jophiel is said to be a close friend of Archangel Metatron.

MACHIDIEL
"Fullness of God"
Color: Pink, yellow

Machidiel (also known as Malchidiel, Malkhidael, Malahidael, and Melkejal) is the archangel of the astrological sign of Aries and rules the month of March. One of the angels of the Tree of Life, he is frequently called upon by people performing love magic. His main concern is to help people gain the necessary courage to be able to express their love to others. Machidiel is sometimes referred to as Prince Machidiel, which might explain why he's usually depicted wearing white clothes and with a small coronet on his head.

METATRON
"The Throne Beside the Throne of God"
Color: White, gold, indigo, violet, green, pink

Metatron was originally Enoch, Adam's great-great-great-great-grandson, who lived on earth for 365 years before being transformed into an angel. (Incidentally, the name "Enoch" means "initiated.") The Bible says: "Enoch walked with God; and he was not, for God took him" (Genesis 5:23–24). When he arrived in heaven, the angels could smell that Enoch was a human; many were unhappy that he'd been turned into an angel. After God answered their objections, he blessed Enoch with 1,365,000 blessings and then enlarged Enoch until he was almost as big as the world. He has thirty-six pairs of wings and 365,000 eyes, each as bright as the sun. Each wing is the size of the world. He and his brother Sandalphon are the tallest angels in heaven.

Because he lived a life as a human before becoming an angel, Metatron is often called the angel of mankind. Metatron is the most important angel in the Jewish tradition. Metatron is also the youngest angel of all, as he was created well after the other angels, who were created on the first day of creation (or maybe even earlier). In the book of Job (38:4–7) the Lord says:

> Where wast thou when I laid the foundations of the earth? Declare, if thou hast understanding. Who hath laid the measures thereof, if thou knowest? Or who hath stretched the line upon it? Whereupon are the foundations thereof fastened? Or who laid the corner stone thereof; when the morning stars sang together, and all the sons of God shouted for joy?

Angels are described as "sons of God" and according to this account, witnessed the creation and even shouted for joy.

Metatron has numerous titles, including Prince of the Presence, Prince of the Countenances, Angel of the Face, Chancellor of Heaven, Master of the Wings, and High Priest of the Heavenly Temple. He's also a member of the sarim and one of the leaders of the seraphim. He's also said to be the angel who teaches the souls of children who died prematurely when they arrive in heaven.

Enoch was famed for his work as a scribe in his earthly life, and is believed to have continued working as God's secretary and archivist in heaven. Unlike all the other angels, he sits upon a beautiful throne located at the entrance to the seventh heaven. Here, Metatron records everything that occurs in the universe, including the sins and good deeds of humanity. These are likely the Akashic records. When Archangel Uriel told him all the secrets of the universe, it took Metatron thirty full days to write it all down; in the process, he filled 360 volumes (Ronner, 103). He is sometimes known as the "Lesser YHWH." YHWH are the four letters of the unspeakable name of God.

The Zohar, the foundational book of Jewish mystical thought known as the Kabbalah, explains that Enoch was chosen to become an angel, having been born with the same divine spark of spiritual perfection Adam had possessed but lost when he was expelled from the Garden of Eden. God couldn't allow someone possessing this divine spark to remain on earth with other mere mortals. Thus, in heaven, Enoch's perfection would be appreciated and used in God's work (1:37b, 1:56b, 1:223b, 2:179a, 3:83b).

In Jewish belief, Metatron carries everyone's prayers directly to God, passing through nine hundred heavens on the way. When the prayers are said in Hebrew, Metatron asks Sandalphon to help him weave the prayer into a garland of flowers that God can wear on his head.

Metatron is said to have helped the tribes of Israel during their forty years in the wilderness. He may have been the angel who wrestled with Jacob, and he possibly stopped Abraham from sacrificing his son Isaac. According to Jewish tradition, Metatron sent Archangel Uriel to warn Noah of the impending flood.

People call on Metatron whenever they need to think deeply, wish to gain more self-esteem, or want to make significant changes in their lives. Metatron is vitally interested in all types of relationships, and can be called upon to help improve work, family, children, and marital relationships. Metatron is highly motivational and enjoys inspiring people into action. He helps people focus on what's really important in their lives. You should call on Metatron when your situation is desperate, and you need a miracle in your life.

MIZRAEL
Color: Pink

Mizrael (also known as Mitzrael) is one of the seventy-two Schemhamphoras, the group of angels who bear the various names of God found in the Jewish scriptures. In the Kabbalah, Mizrael is considered an archangel. She's also a guardian angel for people born between January 26 and February 20.

Mizrael helps creative and talented people develop their skills. She also encourages obedience.

MURIEL
"Fragrance of God"
Color: Pink, white

Muriel is one of the four rulers of the choir of dominions. Muriel also governs the month of June and is responsible for people born under the sign of Cancer. In the *Key of Solomon*, Muriel is said to have power over the south. Occultists claimed that Muriel could be invoked if you wanted to obtain a magic carpet. Muriel usually appears in female form. You can call on Muriel whenever you need to keep your emotions in check.

ORIFIEL
"I order"
Color: Red, indigo

Pope Saint Gregory the Great (540–604 CE) declared Orifiel (also known as Oriphiel, Orifel, and Orfiel) to be one of the seven great archangels alongside Michael, Gabriel, Raphael, Uriel, Simiel (Samael), and Zachariel. Rudolf Steiner agreed with him. However, Orifiel's name doesn't appear in any other listing of archangels. He is considered to be a prince of the choir of thrones, and in the *Lemegeton* (*The Lesser Key of Solomon*), he's called one of the regents of the world. Cornelius Agrippa wrote that Orifiel was a planetary angel, as he looked after the planet Saturn (Agrippa, 535).

Orifiel looks after the fauna and flora of wilderness areas, especially areas uninhabited by humankind. He provides advice and protection to people travelling in remote areas. He also encourages and helps people concerned about nature and the well-being of planet Earth, including ecologists, farmers, and other people who work with the earth but look after it at the same time.

PERPETIEL
Color: White

Though Perpetiel has always been an angel of success, she has been considered an archangel only in recent years, thanks to some New Age angelologists who have increased the list of archangels from seven to twelve. As angels couldn't care less about ranks or titles, this is unlikely to interest Perpetiel, but it has had the advantage of making her better-known.

Perpetiel encourages hope and dreams, and she provides determination and perseverance to help people who are working on worthwhile projects but are finding them hard to accomplish. Perpetiel helps anyone working hard at a worthwhile goal to achieve success. Consequently, Perpetiel is considered an archangel who helps people win against huge odds.

RAGUEL
"Friend of God"
Color: Light blue

According to the second book of Enoch, Raguel (also known as Phanuel, Ragiel, Raguil, and Rufayel) was one of the angels who escorted Enoch to heaven. Raguel maintains discipline in heaven and ensures that all the angels perform their tasks in the best possible way. His duties include justice, harmony, and retribution. He is considered the archangel of justice and fairness. According to 2 Enoch, Raguel and Sariel escorted Enoch to heaven.

Raguel appears as Phanuel in the Ethiopic Book of Parables, where he supervises the repentance of people hoping for everlasting life. He also wards off the forces of evil. This is because the early Hebrews used the name "Phanuel" to provide protection against evil spirits.

The apocryphal Revelation of John says that God will call upon Raguel on Judgment Day after the sheep (good people) have been separated from the goats (bad people): "Then shall He send the angel Raguel, saying: Go, sound the trumpet for the angels of cold and snow and ice, and bring them together every kind of wrath upon them that stand on the left" (the Anti-Nicene Fathers, 586).

Raguel, along with Uriel, Inias, Tubuael, Adimus, Saboath, and Samael, was demoted by Pope Zachary at the council of Rome in 745 CE. At the time, he was concerned that people were worshipping angels rather than God. He kept Michael, Gabriel, and Raphael as they were mentioned in canonical scripture, but condemned the rest. Pope Zachary called Raguel a demon "who passed himself off as a saint." This is a particularly harsh comment about an angel whose task is to look after the other angels and ensure that they don't transgress or behave badly.

Raguel provides strength and persistence to people fighting injustice wherever it is found. He's a peacemaking angel who resolves conflicts and always looks after the underdog. Raguel also helps people resolve their difficulties and enjoy harmonious relationships with others. Raguel helps people seeking partners to find someone who is kind, honest, ethical, and loving.

RAZIEL
"Secret of God"
Color: Yellow, and radiates all the colors of the rainbow

Raziel (also known as Akrasiel, Ratziel, Saraqael, and Suriel) stands behind the curtains in front of the throne of God where he can see and hear everything that is discussed. As a result, he knows all the mysteries of the universe and uses this information to tell humanity the teachings and decrees of God.

Apparently, Raziel felt sorry for Adam and Eve when they were forced out of the Garden of Eden, and gave Adam a magical book called *Sefer Raziel*, or the *Book of the Angel Raziel*. This book contained all the knowledge of the universe and enabled Adam and Eve to create a life for themselves. According to Jewish legend, some of the angels were so unhappy that Adam had gained so much information and wisdom from the book that they stole it and threw it into the ocean. God saw how upset Adam was with this loss and asked Rahab, angel of the sea, to find the book and return it to Adam. Many generations later, Enoch had a dream that told him where the book was located, and he was able to find it again. Thanks to this book, Enoch became the wisest man of his time. Eventually Archangel Raphael gave the book to Noah, who used it to learn how to build his ark. Hundreds of years later, King Solomon used the book to gain wisdom, learn magic, and how to heal others. The book then disappeared until the Middle Ages. The book that was "rediscovered" wasn't the original book, though, and was probably written by a medieval Jewish scholar, such as Eleazar of Worms or Isaac the Blind.

The original book contained the secret to interpreting the 1,500 keys to the mysteries of the world, and Archangel Raziel is said to stand on top of Mount Horeb every day to announce these secrets to all of humanity.

Raziel is said to have blue wings and a large, powerful, yellow aura. He wears a shimmering gray robe. Raziel enjoys helping people create original ideas. Because of his interest in magic, Raziel is willing to help people who wish to develop their psychic abilities, such as clairvoyance, astral travel, and dream interpretation. People can also call on him whenever they have a difficult problem to resolve and are searching for answers. Raziel also helps people who seek abundance in every meaning of the word.

REMIEL
"Mercy of God"
Color: Yellow, purple

Remiel (also known as Ramiel) is the archangel of hope, compassion, divine vision, and dreams. Remiel meets people at the moment of their death and leads their souls up to heaven. She also looks after the souls of the faithful after they have been weighed by Archangel Michael. Remiel helps people who need to see what the future holds for them. In 2 Baruch, one of the books in the Apocrypha, Remiel "presides over true visions" (55:3). In I Enoch, Remiel is said to be one of the seven archangels who attend the throne of God (20:8). Later in the same book, however, Enoch says that Remiel was one of the fallen angels. Although both Remiel and Jeremiel figure many times in religious texts, it's possible that they're both the same archangel, and Remiel is another name for Jeremiel. Remiel and Uriel are the two archangels who have control over thunder.

People call on Remiel when they need peace, harmony, and tranquility in their lives. Remiel also helps people interpret their dreams and visions.

SACHIEL
"Covering of God"
Color: Purple

Sachiel is a member of the choir of cherubim and lives in the first heaven. He is considered the archangel of Jupiter. As Jupiter is the ruling planet of Sagittarius, Sachiel provides help and support for Sagittarians. His day of the week is Thursday.

Sachiel is often invoked regarding legal and financial matters. As the angel of wealth and prosperity, Sachiel is willing to help people to earn money but will not help them obtain money for nothing. As well as helping people earn money and achieve success, Sachiel is also involved in charity and encourages people to be generous and help others less fortunate than they are. He also has a strong interest in politics and spirituality.

The Essenes, a religious sect who were active a hundred years before and after the life of Jesus, believed Sachiel was the angel of water.

SAHAQIEL
"Ingenuity of God"
Color: Green

Sahaqiel is listed in the third book of Enoch as one of the seven great archangels, and rules the sky. He is prince of thrones and looks after the fourth heaven. To do this, he has 496,000 angels to attend and serve him.

Sahaqiel looks after the divine laws to ensure harmony in the universe. When necessary, he acts swiftly to achieve this.

SALAPHIEL
"Communicant of God"
Color: Red

Salaphiel is mentioned as one of the seven ministering angels in the book of Tobit and the book of Esdras. According to the book of Adam and Eve (31:6), Salaphiel and Suriel brought Adam and Eve down from a mountaintop that Satan had lured them to, before taking them to a cave of treasures.

Salaphiel's main task is to encourage and help people to pray. She is willing to help anyone who wants to learn how to pray more effectively. Because of her association with prayer, many Christians believe that she is the angel mentioned in the book of Revelation 8:3–4: "Another angel came and stood at the altar, having a golden censer; and there was given unto her much incense, that she should offer it with the prayers of all saints upon the golden altar which was before the throne. And the smoke of the incense, which came with the prayers of the saints, ascended up before God out of the angel's hand."

SAMAEL
"Severity of God"
Color: Red

Samael (also known as Sammael and Simiel) lives in the seventh heaven but rules the fifth heaven. He is one of the planetary angels and shares the rulership of the planet Mars with Archangel Camael. Both Pope Saint Gregory the Great and Rudolf Steiner considered Samael one of the seven great archangels.

Samael means "blind god." As the word "blind" can mean "ignorant," the ancient Gnostics thought Samael was an evil angel because they associated ignorance with evil. The ancient Jews considered him to be an angel of death. There is another legend to explain Samael's name: Apparently when Moses died, he was reluctant to give up his soul. Samael was asked to retrieve it, and Moses hurt him so badly with his staff that Samael became blind. God had to send Gabriel, Michael, and Zagzagel to help Samael retrieve Moses' soul.

Nowadays, Samael is considered a protective angel who can be called upon whenever people need persistence and courage. Samael helps people deal with their enemies in a gentle manner, enabling them to eliminate long-standing problems.

Samael is said to have twelve wings, and be covered with crystals and precious stones.

SANDALPHON
"Prince of Prayers"
Color: Red, turquoise

Sandalphon (sometimes spelled Sandalfon, Sandolfon, or Sandolphon) is said to be Metatron's twin brother; according to Jewish legend, both led lives on earth before being transformed into angels. This angel's name is possibly derived from two Greek words, *syn*, meaning "together," and *adelphos*, meaning "brother." Consequently, "Sandalphon" means "co-brother."

Sandalphon is said to have been the prophet Elijah when he lived as a human. The Bible says, "Elijah went up by a whirlwind into heaven" in a fiery chariot pulled by two "horses of fire" (2 Kings 2:11). He is believed to be one of the angels of the presence. Sandalphon is best-known for carrying people's prayers to heaven. In Jewish tradition, he weaves garlands of flowers out of Jewish people's prayers, and then charms them to rise and sit on the head of God. He appears to prefer Jewish prayers but is willing to take any prayers up to heaven. Sandalphon's size terrified Moses when he was taken to heaven to receive the Torah; apparently it would take five hundred years to climb from Sandalphon's feet up to the top of his head! He is usually depicted with birds flying around him, and there is usually a sword nearby. This is because he loves all bird life but also acts as one of God's warrior angels. He works closely with Michael in their endless war against Satan.

In Jewish lore, Sandalphon rules the fifth of the seven heavens. However, there are various accounts of where he lives. In rabbinical literature, he's said to live in the third, sixth, and seventh heavens. In Islam, he said to live in the fourth heaven.

In 1858, American poet Henry Wadsworth Longfellow (1807–1882) wrote a poem called "Sandalphon," and in the first verse described Sandalphon as "the angel of glory" and "the angel of prayer."

Sandalphon can be called upon for spiritual advice. He is the archangel of Malkuth in the Kabbalah. Because he also lived on earth, one of his interests is in motivating humans to look after their environments, and according to some legends, it is he who decides whether an unborn baby will be a boy or a girl. Sandalphon is also said to be responsible for all the music in heaven, and encourages people on earth to enjoy the healing benefits of playing and listening to good music, too. Despite his daunting size, Sandalphon has a gentle and loving nature that makes him extremely approachable.

SARIEL
"Command of God"
Color: Red

Sariel is also known as Saraqael, Saraquel, and Zerachiel. In the first book of Enoch, Michael, Sariel, Raphael, and Gabriel looked down on earth from heaven and saw that it "was full of godlessness and violence." This is possibly the earliest mention of the four archangels (Black, 129). Sariel is mentioned by name three times in the book of Enoch (9:1, 10:1, and 20:6). However, almost every other time archangels are mentioned in Enoch's book, Sariel is replaced by Uriel. However, Sariel is not another name for Uriel—both archangels are mentioned in Enoch 20:2–6.

Sariel is one of the angels of the presence, a select group of angels who were created on the first day, according to the book of Jubilees. Sariel is responsible for disciplining any angels who behave badly and also encourages and helps people who want to learn. Sariel is said to be the angel who taught Moses; in Jewish lore, it was Sariel who went to Mount Sinai to retrieve Moses's soul after death. God sent Sariel to Jacob to help him interpret his dream about the ladder. Sariel is one of the angels of healing, and works closely with Raphael in his ministry of healing.

Sariel looks after people born under the sign of Aries. When Sariel is depicted by artists, there is usually an ox in the picture, which is because Sariel is said to appear in the form of an ox.

The Falashas are the oldest and most isolated Jewish community in the world. In a collection of their texts and prayers called the *Falasha Anthology*, Sariel is referred to as both Sariel "the trumpeter" and Sariel "the angel of death."

Sariel is regularly invoked in ceremonial magic, and some people still wear amulets bearing the name of Sariel to protect them from the evil eye. Sariel is said to appear in the form of a powerful ox when invoked.

People ask Sariel for guidance and help when they find life has become too hectic or stressful. He helps people establish and maintain an orderly life. He also brings comfort and hope. People call on Sariel for help with learning and healing. People also communicate with Sariel when facing death or when trying to help someone who is suffering.

SIDRIEL
Color: Pink

According to the third book of Enoch, Sidriel (also known as Padriel and Sabriel) is the archangel in charge of the first heaven. Because of her rank and power, she is assisted by 496,000 angels. He is also ruler of the order of virtues.

SURIEL
"God's Command"
Color: Purple

According to Jewish lore, Suriel (also known as Suruel) taught Moses, and became close to him. Because of this, God sent him down to earth to retrieve Moses's soul after the prophet's death. However, another Jewish legend says that Samael was sent to perform this task. Suriel was listed as one of the four great archangels in the first book of Enoch. Suriel is one of the planetary angels and is responsible for people born under the sign of Taurus.

Suriel is one of the healing angels and can be called upon for any type of spiritual, mental, emotional, or physical healing. Suriel will also provide protection for individuals and groups of people, as well as property and possessions.

VERCHIEL
"Shining of God"
Color: Orange

Verchiel (also known as Zerachiel) is a prince in the choir of Virtues, and one of the rulers of the choir of owers. He is the archangel responsible for the astrological sign of Leo and the month of July.

Because of his association with Leo, Verchiel gives people who are seeking success all the vitality, positivity, and motivation they need to achieve it. Verchiel also provides warmth, affection, friendship, and love. Verchiel resolves difficulties with family members and close friends.

ZACHARIEL
"Remembrance of God"
Color: Blue

Zachariel is listed as one of the great archangels in the first book of Enoch. She also appears in Pope Saint Gregory's list of archangels, and Rudolf Steiner considered her one of the seven great archangels. Zachariel has been listed among the Dominions and Powers as well as a number of lists of archangels. Zachariel is also one of the rulers of the planet Jupiter. In Hebrew lore, Zachariel and Raphael are co-rulers of the second of the seven heavens.

People invoke Zachariel when they need help to improve their concentration and memory. Zachariel is also a healing angel, with a special interest in caring for young children (and their parents).

ZADKIEL
"Righteousness of God"
Color: Violet, indigo, dark blue

In Jewish legend, Zadkiel (also known as Tzadkiel, Zadakiel, and Zedekiel) is best known as being the angel of God who prevented Abraham from sacrificing Isaac. However, several other angels, including Michael, have been credited for this. Despite this, artists almost always depict Zadkiel holding a dagger to remind people of this story.

According to the Zohar, one of the most important books of the Kabbalah, Zadkiel and Jophiel are Michael's two most important companions when he's fighting the forces of evil (Zohar, Numbers 154a). They are standard bearers who are directly behind Michael as he goes into battle.

Zadkiel is prince of the choir of dominions. Pseudo-Dionysius included Zadkiel in his list of seven archangels. Zadkiel is a planetary angel and is ruler of Jupiter. Because of this, Zadkiel has always been associated with generosity, abundance, benevolence, forgiveness, mercy, tolerance, compassion, prosperity, and good fortune, all of which are associated with the planet Jupiter.

People call on Zadkiel when they need more fun and enjoyment in their lives. He provides compassion, love, and understanding. He encourages people to be tolerant and forgiving, both of themselves and others. Zadkiel is also happy to help with legal and financial problems, and is often invoked by people seeking prosperity and abundance. He's also known for helping people improve their memories.

ZAPHKIEL
"Knowledge of God"
Color: Purple

Zaphkiel (also known as Zaphiel, Zephiel, and Zophiel) is prince of the choir of thrones. He is one of the planetary angels who look after the planet of Saturn. However, the ruler of Saturn is Cassiel, leading many people to believe that Zaphkiel is another name for Cassiel. Zaphkiel is often thought to be one of the three unnamed archangels in the Judeo-Christian tradition.

Zaphkiel helps people gain self-understanding and acceptance, and enables them to express unconditional love and compassion for all living things. He encourages forgiveness and compassion, and has a special interest in the well-being of children. He also has an influence on climate and the weather.

ZURIEL
"God Is My Rock"
Color: Green

Zuriel is prince of the choir of principalities. She's also archangel of the sign of Libra and the ruler of September.

Zuriel's main task is to provide harmony and accord. She provides vital energy to people who are feeling run-down and exhausted. Zuriel is an angel of fertility and sexuality. She's also the angel of childbirth and is sometime invoked to help ease the pain of childbirth. Pregnant women used to wear amulets with Zuriel's name inscribed on them to provide protection during childbirth. Zuriel also protects newly born babies. Zuriel heals people suffering from mental health problems and is said to be able to cure stupidity.

Traditionally, Zuriel is known as an archangel of water and provides it for people who are thirsty.

As you can see, archangels have a wide variety of tasks to perform. One of the many responsibilities of Archangels Raphael, Michael, Gabriel, and Uriel is to look after the four elements of air, fire, water, and earth. That is the topic of the next chapter.

How to Invoke
the Archangels

The word "invoke" means to invite or call on a spirit or deity for a specific purpose, such as asking for help, making a request, or giving thanks. Prayers and supplications are effectively invocations. You can invoke any angel you wish, but you'll achieve the best results by invoking angels that are involved with the topic you need help with. You could, for instance, invoke Archangel Michael for help in a love issue, but it would probably be better to call on Archangel Anael for that, as relationship difficulties are not one of Michael's main areas of interest. However, you should definitely invoke him if you need strength or protection.

As we are constantly surrounded by angels and spirit beings, it is not difficult to invoke the angel or archangel you wish to communicate with. The most important part of the process is to be receptive and willing to make the connection. It could be compared to turning on a radio or television. The necessary radio or TV waves are already there, but you're unaware of them until you turn the device on.

You can add strength to your invocation by calling upon the right angel, at the right time, on the right day. You can add further power by using specific colors, crystals, flowers, incense, and candles.

The most commonly invoked angels are: Anael, Cassiel, Chamuel, Gabriel, Metatron, Michael, Raphael, Raziel, Sandalphon, Uriel, and Zadkiel.

ANAEL
Day: Friday
Color: Pink
Crystal: Opal, rose quartz, rhodochrosite
Incense: Lavender
Flower: Red rose
Candle: Pink

Anael is invoked for any matters relating to friendship, love, romance, sexuality, harmony, and peace of mind.

CASSIEL
Day: Saturday
Color: White
Crystal: Hematite, obsidian, onyx
Incense: Myrrh
Flower: Eucalyptus
Candle: White

You can invoke Cassiel for any matters involving moderation, stability, patience, karma, and serenity.

CHAMUEL
Day: Tuesday
Color: Red
Crystal: Bloodstone, carnelian, fluorite, ruby
Incense: Cinnamon
Flower: Red carnation
Candle: Red

You can invoke Chamuel for any matters relating to friendship and love, and your home and work lives. Chamuel will also help you resolve any problems you have in your dealings with others.

GABRIEL
Day: Monday
Color: White, silver, violet
Crystal: Moonstone, selenite
Incense: Jasmine
Flower: White lilies, violets
Candle: Silver

You can invoke Archangel Gabriel for any matters involving messages and communication. Gabriel is also willing to help in any matters involving children, from conception to adulthood. Gabriel can also be invoked to overcome any self-destructive tendencies, such as procrastination.

METATRON
Day: Any day
Color: White
Crystal: Diamond
Incense: Frankincense
Flower: White flowers
Candle: White

Metatron can be invoked for any matters involving spiritual growth and development. He is particularly interested in helping children and young adults develop their spiritual awareness.

MICHAEL
Day: Sunday
Color: Blue, purple, gold
Crystal: Citrine, sugilite, sunstone, topaz
Incense: Frankincense
Flower: Marigold
Candle: Gold, blue, purple, or red

You can invoke Archangel Michael for any matters involving truth, courage, and protection. He can also help you find your purpose in this lifetime. Michael can be called upon for any purpose at all. Usually people call on him when in need of urgent help, but he's frequently invoked to help with mechanical and technical problems, as well.

RAPHAEL
Day: Wednesday
Color: Green, yellow
Crystal: Agate, amazonite, aventurine, chrysoprase,
emerald, green jade, green jasper, malachite
Incense: Copal
Flower: Yellow and orange flowers
Candle: Orange

You can call on Archangel Raphael for any matters relating to healing and travel. Raphael can be invoked for help in all forms of healing, including pets and other animals, as well as people. Many people ask Raphael for help and safety when planning a trip.

RAZIEL
Day: Any day
Color: Yellow plus all the colors of the rainbow
Crystal: Clear quartz
Incense: Sandalwood

Flower: Brightly colored flowers
Candle: Yellow

You can call upon Raziel whenever you need help in understanding your dreams, recalling past-life memories, developing rituals, self-empowering yourself, and all forms of esoteric study.

SANDALPHON
Day: Any day
Color: Red, turquoise
Crystal: Smoky quartz, turquoise
Incense: Sandalwood
Flower: Carnation, ivy, lily
Candle: White

You can invoke Archangel Sandalphon for help in eliminating anxieties, fears, and worries. He may recommend that you listen to certain types of music to help you gain a sense of positivity and optimism.

URIEL
Day: Friday
Color: Red, yellow, orange, blue
Crystal: Amethyst, aquamarine, aventurine,
bloodstone, carnelian, tourmaline
Incense: Patchouli
Flower: Orchids
Candle: Red, yellow, orange, or blue

Archangel Uriel can be invoked whenever you find yourself in a difficult situation and need help to resolve it. Uriel will help you to think clearly and logically. Uriel is also willing to help people who are studying to retain the information they have learned.

ZADKIEL

Day: Thursday
Color: Violet
Crystal: Azurite, lapis lazuli, turquoise
Incense: Sandalwood
Flower: Gladiolus
Candle: Violet, dark blue

Archangel Zadkiel works with Archangel Uriel to help people remember what they've learned.

THE RIGHT DAY

You can and should contact the angel of your choosing as soon as the need arises. Consequently, you can create an invocation ritual to be used whenever you wish. However, if the actual day is not of paramount importance, you should use days that relate to your own personal vibration. The best day for you to contact a particular angel might not necessarily be the best day for someone else. This is because your personal rate of vibration is determined by the day of the month you were born on. There are three groups of personal vibrations:

You belong to Group One if you were born on the 1st, 5th, 7th, 10th, 14th, 16th, 19th, 23rd, 25th, or 28th day of the month.

You belong to Group Two if you were born on the 2nd, 4th, 8th, 11th, 13th, 17th, 20th, 22nd, 26th, 29th, or 31st day of the month.

You belong to Group Three if you were born on the 3rd, 6th, 9th, 12th, 15th, 18th, 21st, 24th, 27th, or 30th day of the month.

The best days for you each month are divided into spiritual, mental, and physical. The spiritual days are the best days to contact an archangel for all forms of healing and spiritual matters. The mental days are the best days to invoke an archangel for any matters involving your mind, e.g., difficulties at home and matters relating to work, study, or the people you encounter. The physical days are the best days to invoke an archangel for any matters involving growth or increase, including business dealings and financial matters.

Group One

1st day of the month:

Spiritual: 1st, 5th, and 7th.
Mental: 10th, 14th, 16th, and 19th.
Physical: 23rd, 25th, and 28th.

5th day of the month:

Spiritual: 7th, 10th, and 14th.
Mental: 16th, 19th, 23rd, and 25th.
Physical: 1st, 5th, and 28th.

7th day of the month:

Spiritual: 10th, 14th, 16th, and 19th.
Mental: 23rd, 25th, and 28th.
Physical: 1st, 5th, and 7th.

10th day of the month:

Spiritual: 16th, 19th, 23rd, and 25th.
Mental: 1st, 5th, and 28th.
Physical: 7th, 10th, and 14th.

14th day of the month:

Spiritual: 23rd, 25th, and 28th.
Mental: 1st, 5th, and 7th.
Physical: 10th, 14th, and 16th.

16th day of the month:

Spiritual: 5th, 7th, and 10th.
Mental: 14th, 16th, 19th, and 23rd.
Physical: 1st, 25th, and 28th.

19th day of the month:

Spiritual: 7th, 10th, 14th, and 16th.
Mental: 19th, 23rd, 25th, and 28th.
Physical: 1st and 5th.

23rd day of the month:

Spiritual: 14th, 16th, 19th, and 23rd.
Mental: 1st, 25th, and 28th.
Physical: 5th, 7th, and 10th.

25th day of the month:

Spiritual: 19th, 23rd, 25th, and 28th.
Mental: 1st and 5th.
Physical: 7th, 10th, 14th, and 16th.

28th day of the month:

Spiritual: 1st, 25th, and 28th.
Mental: 5th, 7th, and 10th.
Physical: 14th, 16th, 19th, and 23rd.

Group Two

2nd day of the month:

Spiritual: 2nd, 4th, 8th, and 11th.
Mental: 13th, 17th, 20th, and 22nd.
Physical: 26th, 29th, and 31st

4th day of the month:

> Spiritual: 8th, 11th, 13th, and 17th.
> Mental: 20th, 22nd, 26th, and 29th.
> Physical: 2nd, 4th, and 31st.

8th day of the month:

> Spiritual: 13th, 17th, 20th, and 22nd.
> Mental: 26th, 29th, and 31st.
> Physical: 2nd, 4th, 8th, and 11th.

11th day of the month:

> Spiritual: 20th, 22nd, 26th, and 29th.
> Mental: 2nd, 4th, and 31st.
> Physical: 8th, 11th, 13th, and 17th.

13th day of the month:

> Spiritual: 26th, 29th, and 31st.
> Mental: 2nd, 4th, 8th, and 11th.
> Physical: 13th, 17th, 20th, and 22nd.

17th day of the month:

> Spiritual: 4th, 8th, 11th, and 13th.
> Mental: 17th, 20th, 22nd, and 26th.
> Spiritual: 2nd, 29th, and 31st.

20th day of the month:

> Spiritual: 11th, 13th, 17th, and 20th.
> Mental: 22nd, 26th, 29th, and 31st.
> Physical: 2nd, 4th, and 8th.

22nd day of the month:

> Spiritual: 17th, 20th, 22nd, and 26th.
> Mental: 2nd, 29th, and 31st.
> Physical: 4th, 8th, 11th, and 13th.

26th day of the month:

> Spiritual: 22nd, 26th, 29th, and 31st.
> Mental: 2nd, 4th, and 8th.
> Physical: 11th, 13th, 17th, and 20th.

29th day of the month:

> Spiritual: 2nd, 29th, and 31st.
> Mental: 4th, 8th, 11th, and 13th.
> Physical: 17th, 20th, 22nd, and 26th.

31st day of the month:

> Spiritual: 2nd, 4th, and 31st.
> Mental: 8th, 11th, 13th, and 17th.
> Physical: 20th, 22nd, 26th, and 31st.

Group Three

3rd day of the month:

> Spiritual: 3rd, 6th, 9th, and 12th.
> Mental: 15th, 18th, 21st, and 24th.
> Physical: 27th and 30th.

6th day of the month:

> Spiritual: 9th, 12th, 15th, and 18th.
> Mental: 21st, 24th, 27th, and 30th.
> Physical: 3rd and 6th.

9th day of the month:

> Spiritual: 15th, 18th, 21st, and 24th.
> Mental: 27th and 30th.
> Physical: 3rd, 6th, 9th, and 12th.

12th day of the month:

> Spiritual: 21st, 24th, 27th, and 30th.
> Mental: 3rd and 6th.
> Physical: 9th, 12th, 15th, and 18th.

15th day of the month:

> Spiritual: 27th and 30th.
> Mental: 3rd, 6th, 9th, and 12th.
> Physical: 15th, 18th, 21st, and 24th.

18th day of the month:

> Spiritual: 6th, 9th, 12th, and 15th.
> Mental: 18th, 21st, 24th, and 27th.
> Physical: 3rd and 30th.

21st day of the month:

> Spiritual: 12th, 15th, 18th, and 21st.
> Mental: 24th, 27th, and 30th.
> Physical: 3rd, 6th, and 9th.

24th day of the month:

> Spiritual: 18th, 21st, 24th, and 27th.
> Mental: 3rd and 30th.
> Physical: 6th, 9th, 12th, and 15th.

27th day of the month:

> Spiritual: 24th, 27th, and 30th.
> Mental: 3rd, 6th, and 9th.
> Physical: 12th, 15th, 18th, and 21st.

30th day of the month:

> Spiritual: 3rd and 30th.
> Mental: 6th, 9th, 12th, and 15th.
> Physical: 18th, 21st, 24th, and 27th.

THE INVOCATION

You now know everything necessary to perform an invocation to your chosen archangel.

Required:

- A table to act as an altar
- A chair
- A glass of wine (the drink need not be alcoholic; fruit juice or a glass of water also work well)
- A dinner roll, a slice of bread, or a handful of unsalted nuts
- 2 candles in the archangel's color (if you cannot find candles in the color specified, use white candles)
- Incense, a crystal, flower, and an attractive item that features the chosen archangel's color

Whenever possible, perform the invocation at a time when the moon is waxing on a day that relates to your personal vibrations. You might also be able to perform the ritual at the angel's correct planetary hour (see chapter nine).

1. Have a leisurely bath or shower, and put on clean, loose-fitting clothes.

2. Place all the necessary items on your altar.

3. Light the candles and the incense.

4. Construct a circle of protection around yourself and your altar.

5. Face east and spread your arms out wide. Say something along the lines of:

   Archangel (name), I invite you into my circle, as I desperately need help with (explain exactly what the concern is). Please bring me the benefit of your knowledge and wisdom. I ask this in the name of Universal Spirit (Architect of the Universe, God, or whatever name you choose), whom I believe in and trust implicitly. I know I am loved and cared for. Please accept these humble offerings and help me resolve this problem. Thank you. Thank you. Thank you.

6. Wait quietly with your arms spread until you sense that the archangel is with you. Say one more "thank you," and sit down on the chair.

7. Eat the food and drink the wine.

8. Stand up and face east. Close the circle.

Repeat this ritual at least seven times over the following two months. Ideally, this should be done about once a week at the angel's correct planetary hour (see chapter nine). If this isn't practical for you, perform the ritual at the same time once a week for a seven-week period.

In the next chapter, we'll look at a number of different techniques and rituals that you can use when working with the archangels.

CHAPTER SEVEN

WORKING WITH THE ARCHANGELS

You can work with the archangels in many different ways. You'll find several techniques and rituals in this chapter, starting with a deceptively simple way to attract the qualities of a particular archangel to you.

POSITIVE QUALITIES

With practice, you'll be able to perform this ritual in a matter of seconds whenever you need guidance or help in any area of your life.

1. Start by choosing the particular archangel you need. If you don't know who you need specifically, you can in fact ask any archangel to help you. For example, if someone has hurt you, call on any archangel you wish to help you forgive the other person. Each archangel puts their own particular slant on the process. It might be easier to choose an angel from the listing in the appendix for different purposes. Continuing with our example, assume you're finding it difficult to forgive someone for something they did to you. Under "Forgiveness," you'll find four archangels who regularly

help people to forgive others: Chamuel, Jeremiel, Zadkiel, and Zaphiel. Of these, let's assume you choose Chamuel.

2. Sit down somewhere comfortable and close your eyes. Visualize Archangel Chamuel standing in front of you. You can visualize Chamuel in any way you wish. You might "see" a larger-than-life person, a traditional-looking angel with large wings, or perhaps a large ball of colorful energy. It's just as likely you'll "see" nothing but instead have a sense that Chamuel is standing directly in front of you.

3. Once you know that Archangel Chamuel is with you, tell him you need help to forgive the other person. Inhale deeply, and feel your body filling with Chamuel's energy. Do this twice more, and thank Chamuel for his help.

4. Say goodbye to Chamuel. Open your eyes, and carry on with your day.

You'll probably find that after performing this ritual, you'll be able to forgive the person unreservedly. If necessary, repeat the ritual several times a day until your feelings about the other person are neutral and the forgiveness is complete.

With practice, you'll be able to perform this ritual anywhere, at any time, with eyes open. If you use this ritual for a variety of purposes, you'll become familiar with a wide range of archangels that you'll be able to work with whenever you need help.

PRAYER

The word "prayer" comes from the Latin *precari*, which means "to beseech or implore." Throughout history, prayer has been used to ask for things for ourselves and others. The desire to communicate with the Divine is universal and still a popular practice. A 2014 US Religious Landscape Study found that 55 percent of Americans pray every day (https://www.pewforum.org/religious-landscape-study/frequency-of-prayer/).

You don't have to get down on bended knees to pray. You can pray at any time, no matter where you are. You can pray while sitting or lying down, walking, or driving in your car. You can pray while waiting in line. An acquaintance of mine prays while working out on a treadmill.

There is no need to use formal or flowery language when you pray. Your intent is more important than the words you use. A simple, heartfelt prayer will always be effective.

You can include any angel or archangel in your prayers. You can ask your guardian angel to deliver your prayers for you, or you might ask the specific angel or archangel who has an involvement in the topic of your prayer to deliver it for you. (A listing of the different purposes and the archangels who can help you resolve problems and difficulties can be found in the appendix.)

You can also ask specific archangels to pray with you. However, if you haven't worked with a particular archangel before, you'll find it easier if you spend some time together first.

HOW TO GAIN ANGELIC AWARENESS

Set aside some time when you won't be disturbed. Sit down in a comfortable chair, close your eyes, and relax. Some people lie down when performing this exercise; you might find it more relaxing to do it that way, rather than sitting in a chair. I always sit in a chair, as I fall asleep far too easily when I'm lying down.

Focus on your breathing and take ten slow, deep breaths. Each time you inhale, hold your breath for a few seconds, and then exhale slowly while silently saying to yourself, "relax, relax, relax." After ten breaths, forget about your breathing. Mentally scan your body, from the tips of your toes to the top of your head to make sure that you're completely relaxed. Focus on any areas of tension until they loosen and you feel totally relaxed.

Enjoy the peace and quiet for a few moments. If you've ever experienced a magical or mystical moment when you felt at one with the world, you'll recognize the sensation immediately and know that you've raised your vibration. Angels have a higher vibration than we do; consequently, we need to raise our vibration to communicate with them effectively.

In this nice, calm, relaxed state, think about your need to communicate with a specific angel or archangel. Send thoughts of love and gratitude to this archangel and offer thanks for their presence and for listening to you. Explain why you want to make contact, and ask if they'll help you. Pause and wait for a response. The response may come as a feeling that the archangel is with you. You might sense a gentle touch, notice a change of temperature in the room, or hear a slight, unexplainable sound. Be aware of any changes that occur, as it could be a message. If you're particularly fortunate, the response may come in words that seem to come from directly beside your ear or even from inside your head. You'll know right away that these are not random thoughts—the voice will seem more vibrant and loving, and the messages you receive will provide you with information and insights that you wouldn't otherwise know.

You might be fortunate and receive a response right away. If this happens, express your thanks and ask the archangel for any advice or help he can give you. Don't worry if you don't experience anything on your first, second, or even tenth attempt. You may have lived on earth for many years without trying to contact an archangel. The angel might be testing you to see if you'll try once and give up, or if you're serious and will continue working until you do make contact.

Remain positive if you don't receive a response. Repeat the exercise regularly, and sooner or later it will happen. It's possible that you'll receive a response when you're not performing the exercise. It may come in the form of a dream. You may wake up one morning and have the information you need.

Dreams can be hard to remember, especially if you're woken up by an alarm clock. On a normal day, we jump out of bed and the dream is forgotten in a matter of seconds. If possible, remain in the position you were in when you woke up, and recall as much of the dream as you can. Only then, change position or get out of bed. As soon as you can, record the dream in some sort of way. You might write it down or record it into your phone. As you've now unlocked the dream, more thoughts about the dream are likely to come to you during the day, and you'll be able to add them to your record. Later, when you have time, analyze the dream to see what message it's telling you. The quality of the message will tell you if it's from an archangel.

You may also receive messages in the form of signs. A lady I know experiences a beautiful scent that tells her she's made an angelic connection. At a talk I gave many years ago, a lady told me that she experiences a strange, high-pitched whistling sound. I sometimes find small denomination coins or white feathers, and know that they're messages from the angelic kingdom.

You may find that the problem you wanted to discuss with an archangel is suddenly (usually unexpectedly) resolved. This means that the archangel has manipulated the situation and created a solution that is fair to everyone concerned.

After you've established contact once, you'll find you'll be able to connect with whichever angel you need to communicate with whenever you wish. I think it is a matter partly related to confidence. If you haven't made contact with angels before, there's always a feeling of doubt that you won't be able to connect. But once you've successfully contacted the angelic realms once, you'll be confident that you'll be able to do it again. Consequently, don't feel disappointed and give up if you fail to make a connection right away.

I enjoy performing the ritual of sitting down, closing my eyes, and taking ten slow, deep breaths. Once you've made a number of successful contacts, you'll find that you can establish it instantly wherever you happen to be. If you travel by public transport, for instance, you could make angelic contact while on the bus or train. You might spend a few minutes at work communicating with an archangel. You can do the same thing while waiting in line, when stuck in traffic, or waiting to fall asleep.

Some people like to record a guided visualization for themselves to help them raise their vibration and get into the ideal state for an angelic communication. The following is a script that will help you relax enough to reach this state.

Take a nice deep breath, and close your eyes as you exhale. Each breath takes you deeper and deeper. Feel yourself relaxing more and more with each easy breath you take, as you drift into a nice, calm, peaceful, totally relaxed state. Nothing need bother or disturb you. It's effortless and easy to do. I'd like you to take three deep breaths, and on the third breath hold it for the count of three. Each time you exhale, say to yourself "relax, relax, relax," and you'll find this will take you even deeper into pleasant relaxation. Take the first deep breath. Relaxation coming in, and tension and stress flowing out. That's good, very good. Take the second big breath, and feel the relaxion coming in and the tension and stress flowing out. And now, the third deep breath. Relaxation coming in, hold it for the count of three—one, two, three—and exhale. Allow yourself to feel loose, limp, and so, so relaxed.

Feel the relaxation in your toes and feet, and then let the relaxation drift up into your legs. Allow the pleasant relaxation to flow into your abdomen, and then, let it move up into your chest and shoulders. When you feel ready, let the relaxation drift down your arms and into your hands and fingers. Allow this wonderful relaxation to move into your neck and face, and flow right up to the top of your head. Think of your eyes now, and let the muscles around your eyes relax even more.

Enjoy the relaxation for a few moments, and then mentally scan your body to make sure that every cell is completely relaxed. When you feel that every part of you is totally relaxed, imagine you're surrounded by angels: they're all there because they love you and want you to enjoy the very best that life has to offer.

Think of your need to speak to a specific angel. You need only think of this angel and they'll appear. Thank this angel for everything they've done for you, and make your request. Tell them everything you can about your need, and, when you've finished, thank them for listening. (Remain silent for two or three minutes.)

Thank the angel again, and say goodbye. Thank all the angels who have been surrounding you and sending you love and support. Ask them for an angelic blessing. Thank them again for everything they do for you, and say goodbye. When you feel ready, count slowly from one to five, and open your eyes.

You might need to experiment with the script to make sure that you're allowing enough time to perform everything necessary you want. You might find that you need more than a few minutes to discuss everything you want to cover with the particular angel. The script should be adjusted to suit you and your needs. You certainly don't want to rush through the relaxation process, as it's important to feel totally relaxed before communicating with the angels.

Set aside enough time to play your recording and still have time to lie quietly for a few minutes afterward to think about the experience. Have something to eat and drink before doing anything else.

WALKING MEDITATION

I enjoy walking and go for a walk almost every day. I often ask an angel to join me. I usually walk with my guardian angel but call on other angels and archangels when I feel the need. After walking for about five minutes, I ask the particular angel I want to talk with to join me. After a minute or two, I'll become aware that the angel is walking with me. I don't hear or see the angel but experience a strong sense of their presence. We'll walk in silence for about a minute, and then I'll start talking with the angel.

If I'm out in the country, I'll talk out loud, but I've learned that it's better to do this silently while walking along city streets. It probably wouldn't matter nowadays, as every second person I encounter is talking on their cellphone, but I prefer to speak to the angels out loud only when I'm on my own. The angel's replies appear as thoughts in my mind. Once we've discussed everything I want or need to know, I'll thank the angel, say goodbye, and finish the walk on my own.

Once you've become used to doing this, you'll find that you can walk with an angel anywhere, even in a busy shopping mall.

WRITING TO AN ARCHANGEL

Writing a letter to an archangel is an extremely useful way to communicate. You need to put time, thought, and energy into writing a letter, and this concentrates your energies. More ideas will come to you as you write, and you might receive a solution to the problem while you're still writing the letter. When this occurs, I believe that the archangel gave me the solution. An archangel would obviously be aware of what I was doing as soon as I put pen to paper, maybe even earlier. From their unlimited vantage point, they'd be able to see many solutions that would never have occurred to me, and it would be a simple matter for them to put those solutions into my mind. On other occasions, you'll find you're communicating with the archangel while writing the letter and will be able to put the letter aside and have a talk about the problem or concern.

Write the letter as if you're communicating with a good friend—in fact, this is what you are doing. There's no need to use formal language. While you're writing, include some information about yourself, your life, and hopes and dreams. Finish the letter by thanking the archangel for what has been and is being done for you. Express your love, and sign your name. Once the letter is finished, seal it in an envelope, and write the archangel's name on the front.

The final step is to "post" or "send" the letter. Light a candle (preferably a white one) and sit in front of it while holding the letter in your cupped hands. Think about what you've written in the letter and thank the archangel for taking care of the problem for you. Once you've said everything you wish to say, thank him again, and then burn the envelope and its contents in the candle flame. Watch the smoke carry your message up to the angelic realms. Say a final thank-you and carry on with your day, confident that the archangel will be taking care of your concern.

Naturally, you need to be careful when doing anything with candles. I place my candles on metal trays and always have a container of water close at hand. I've never had any problems, but it makes me feel happier knowing that I've taken precautions, just in case a candle falls over, or anything else untoward happens.

You might find that you enjoy communicating with the angelic realms with words on paper. If you do, you'll find it helpful to write a journal with your angels. Start by writing anything that occurs to you; it doesn't matter what it happens to be. You might write about something pleasant you're planning to do or maybe what you're going to prepare for dinner. The purpose is to clear your mind. When the time seems right, or when you run out of things to say, start a new page by writing, "Dear (whatever angel you wish to speak with), do you have a message for me?" Pause and see if anything comes into your mind. Write down everything that comes through. Once you start, the writing will flow and the process will seem effortless.

AFFIRMATIONS

Affirmations are positive phrases or words that are repeated regularly until the message is clearly imprinted into the subconscious mind. We all have thousands of thoughts every day, and have no idea how many of them are positive and how many are negative. You can increase the number of positive thoughts by deliberately saying constructive affirmations that relate to whatever it is you want.

Affirmations work because they create energy that over time changes your body and mind at a cellular level. Medical science has known for many years that negative thinking can ultimately create psychosomatic illnesses. Our thoughts have the ability to change the mental state of others, too. If you spend much time with someone who is angry or unhappy, you're likely to pick up their negative energy and start feeling unhappy too. Fortunately, the opposite also applies: when you're with someone who's full of all the joys of life, you'll absorb that energy and feel more positive and happier than you were before you met the other person.

Affirmations are always framed in the present tense, as if you already have whatever it is that you desire. You might affirm "I am a good listener," even if that has never been the case in the past. This is not dishonesty, as everything begins with a thought, and your affirmation is the spark that enables that thought to ultimately become your reality.

Phrase your affirmations in a positive way to affirm what you want, rather than what you don't want. You'll receive better results if you affirm "I think before I buy," rather than "I no longer overspend."

Affirmations can be spoken out loud, whispered, sung, or said silently. You can also write them down. It's important that they're said with feeling, as if they were already an integral part of your life. I like to say my affirmations when driving by myself in the car. This means I can say them out loud and can place the emphasis on different words each time I repeat them. I say my affirmations silently whenever I'm waiting in line. I also like saying my affirmations while standing in front of a mirror. It can be an interesting experiment to say something positive and complimentary to your reflection, and to then follow that with your affirmations.

I thoroughly enjoy writing my affirmations down. I write the same affirmation at least ten times on a sheet of paper. While writing it, I can see the words appear, and can silently say them to myself at the same time. Once I've written the affirmation at least ten times, I'll fold the sheet of paper and keep it with me in my wallet or in a pocket, so that I can read it whenever I have a few spare moments.

At the start of the twentieth century, French psychotherapist Emile Coué (1857–1926) became an international celebrity with a powerful affirmation that helped thousands of people. It was: "Every day and in every way, I am becoming better and better." This is an example of a general affirmation. Here are two more general affirmations that I find useful: "I deserve the very best that life has to offer," and "I'm alive, I'm well, and I feel great!"

You can create affirmations for any purpose. If, for instance, you wanted to attract money, you might say, "I have more money than I need." If you wanted to gain friends, you could say, "I have plenty of friends."

Affirmations can be used to improve every aspect of your life, including your spiritual life. They are a quick and effective way to make and maintain contact with the angelic realms.

All you need do is think of your need, decide on the archangel you think would be best to help you with it, and create an affirmation using this information. Short affirmations are usually better than long ones. A simple example might be: "Archangel Raphael heals me."

Here are some more examples:

Archangel Raphael heals me spiritually, emotionally, mentally, and physically.

Archangel Michael fills me with confidence and strength.

Archangel Gabriel surrounds my soul with peace and love.

Archangel Uriel provides me with peace and tranquility.

I am open to the flow of Raphael's healing energy.

Today I listen to the advice of Archangel...

I open my heart to the blessings of the angels.

I am open to receive love and guidance from the angels.

I am constantly surrounded by angels who watch over and protect me.

Once you start working with affirmations, you'll discover that repeating them whenever you have a spare moment, as well as when you have the need to speak to a specific angel, will increase your connection with the entire angelic realms, as well as the angel you want to connect with.

CANDLE MEDITATION

I've always enjoyed working with candles and find them extremely useful when it comes to working with the angelic realms. I like to perform this ritual in the evening when there is no light except for the candle flame.

You can use any candle you wish. I have a large collection of different colored candles, and usually know what color candle I'll use well before starting the ritual. I keep my candles in a drawer and sometimes leave the choice up to chance, using whatever candle my hand touches first. At other times, I'll choose a particular candle based on the specific angel I'm working with, the meanings of the different colors, and my particular need at the time. Here are the usual color associations:

Red provides confidence, vitality, enthusiasm, and energy.

Orange provides motivation and self-esteem while eliminating fear, doubt, and worry.

Yellow stimulates the mind and helps with open, honest communication. It provides joy and happiness.

Green relieves stress, impatience, and anger. It also provides stability, self-worth, and contentment.

Blue provides serenity and wholeness. It also helps overcome nervousness and indecision.

Indigo provides faith, love, and support. It also helps you handle family problems.

Violet provides spirituality, intuition, inner peace, and nurtures the soul.

Pink helps in overcoming emotional difficulties and helps you give and receive love.

Gray helps overcome mental exhaustion.

Silver provides inspiration, confidence, and self-esteem.

Gold provides positive feelings about achievement, success, and financial improvement.

White provides purity, protection, and spirituality.

Black provides change, freedom, new starts, and sophistication.

You can use a white candle for any purpose. If you're not sure which candle to use, choose a white one.

Place a lit candle on a table about six feet away from where you'll be sitting. The flame of the candle should be at about the level of your third eye when you're sitting down.

Sit down, take a few slow, deep breaths, and gaze at the flickering flame. This is extremely relaxing, and you'll soon find your eyes wanting to close. Resist the urge, and think of your need to contact whatever archangel you want to talk with. After a few minutes, you're likely to sense or even catch a glimpse of an archangel. When this happens, start talking with the angel, silently or out loud.

Again, always be careful when working with candles. Anything to do with fire has the potential to be dangerous. I place my candles on a metal tray and always have a jug of water nearby. A friend of mine has a small fire extinguisher.

I've been performing this ritual for more than forty years and almost always experience the presence of the angel I need to talk with. However, there are times when I don't make contact with the angel I want to speak with or any other angel. When this happens, I simply gaze at the candle for a few more minutes and breathe in the color association of whatever candle I'm using, allowing it to fill my body with its special energy. After I've done that, I thank the angel I was trying to contact, snuff out the candle, and carry on with my day. I don't worry about why the angel didn't appear or think that I had somehow failed to make the connection. I assume that the angel was busy helping someone else and perform the ritual again a day or two later.

CIRCLE OF JOY

The circle of joy is a magic circle that you create around yourself. It's a special, sacred space approximately seven feet in diameter that you can perform any type of spiritual work within. You can create the circle in a number of different ways. I used to have a length of cord to create the circle. I've also made the circle by using small objects such as crystals, stones, or small ornaments. If you're working with someone else, you might create the circle using lit candles. However, as this is potentially dangerous, you should never do this when working on your own. I also have a large circular rug that I use when performing my rituals indoors. With practice, you'll be able to imagine a circle around yourself, but it's better to start with a physical circle to help you become familiar with the size required.

Once you've created your circle, place a comfortable chair in the center. Walk around the circle a few times and then sit down comfortably in the chair. Close your eyes, take five or six slow, deep breaths, and imagine a beautiful white light descending from the sky and filling you and your circle with protection. You'll feel safe, secure, and protected inside your circle of joy. It's a quiet, special, sacred place that you can visit whenever you feel the need to relax and destress, think things through, or communicate with the angelic realms.

When you feel ready, ask the particular archangel you want to communicate with to join you inside the circle of joy. Sit quietly and feel happy, as you know the angel will soon be with you. When the angel arrives, thank them for joining you and start a conversation. You'll feel totally free to discuss anything at all, and you'll have as much time as you need to cover everything on your mind. When the conversation is over, thank the archangel for helping you and say goodbye.

Sit quietly in the circle with your eyes closed for another minute or two. You can sit for longer if you wish. When you feel ready, open your eyes. Stand up, stretch, and step outside the circle when you feel ready.

One of the wonderful benefits of having your own circle of joy is that you can create it whenever you wish, wherever you happen to be. You can create your own peaceful haven whenever you feel the need for safety, protection, and divine love. It's also the perfect environment to communicate with the angelic realms.

CIRCLE OF PROTECTION

This ritual is a more advanced version of the circle of joy. It incorporates Raphael, Michael, Gabriel, and Uriel—the four great archangels. You'll find it will help you enormously in every area of your life. Ideally, you should master the circle of joy ritual before experimenting with this one. The circle of protection is based on the Lesser Banishing Ritual of the Pentagram (called the LBRP for short) that was created and used by members of the Hermetic Order of the Golden Dawn, a secret order that transformed magic in the late nineteenth and early twentieth centuries.

If possible, you should have a shower or bath before performing the circle of protection. This symbolically purifies you. You might like to change into loose-fitting clothes (e.g., robes) to further separate yourself from your everyday life.

Use a rope or a selection of small objects to create a circle. Alternatively, visualize the circle in your mind. Depending on whatever it is you intend doing inside the circle, you might like to place a chair in the center and create the circle around it.

Stand in the center of your circle and face east. This is easy to do nowadays, as almost everyone has a compass on their cellphones. Close your eyes and imagine white light descending from the heavens. Visualize it filling you and your magic circle with divine protection. When you sense that you are completely surrounded by white light, say "thank you" out loud.

You're now ready to call on the four great archangels. Open your eyes and visualize Raphael standing directly in front of you. People "see" the archangels in different ways. You might see him as a bearded, robed figure holding a staff in one hand and a fish in the other. This is how Raphael is usually depicted. It's more likely that you'll sense him as energy or a rainbow of color. As he represents the element of air, you might visualize him as a strong gust of wind. It makes no difference how you experience him—or her, for that matter—just as long as you know Raphael is there. When you first start experimenting with this, you might have to imagine he's there. Once you sense that Raphael is in front of you, extend your right arm and hand, with the first two fingers extended, directly in front of you. Starting from your left hip, draw a large, vivid blue pentagram (five-pointed star) in the air, moving your hand from your left hip to the center of your forehead, down to your right hip, up to your left shoulder, across to your right shoulder, and back down to your left hip. Once you've done this, bring your hand back a few inches and then make a stabbing motion through the center of this pentagram.

Keep your right hand extended as you turn ninety degrees to face south. Visualize a pure white light that appears to be drawn as you move to face south. This time, visualize Michael as clearly as you can. Again, you might see him as a bearded figure holding a set of scales, wielding a sword, and with one foot resting on a dragon. Alternatively, he might appear as whirls of color or light. Many people "see" him as a huge, blazing fire, as he represents the element of fire. Once you sense he's there, draw another blue pentagram, finishing by making a stabbing motion in the center. With your arm still extended, turn another ninety degrees to face west, drawing a pure white line as you turn. This time, visualize Gabriel holding a trumpet and a lily. As Gabriel represents the element of water, you might see her as a blue mist to symbolize water. Once you have a clear picture in your mind, make a vivid blue pentagram in the air, stab it, and then create another white line as you turn to face north. This time visualize Uriel. He's usually depicted with a scroll in one hand and a burning flame on the other. Once you have him clearly in mind, construct a final pentagram, stab it, and create a white line as you turn to face east again.

You are now completely surrounded by the four great archangels and can perform anything you wish inside your circle, knowing that you are completely protected. Thank the archangels for their help and protection and discuss anything you wish with them. You can also pray to the Divine, ask to communicate with any member of the angelic kingdom you wish, and then have a conversation with them, all while you're in the circle.

When you're ready to close your circle and carry on with your day, face east once more and thank Raphael for his love and care. Turn to the south and thank Michael, followed by Gabriel and Uriel. Finally, face east again, say thank you in any way that seems appropriate, and step out of the circle.

You do not need to repeat the opening ritual to remove the pentagrams. By performing the ritual, you have absorbed them into your being, and they'll provide you with a sense of security and protection.

This ceremony can be an emotional one. Allow as much time as necessary before carrying on with your day. You'll find the circle of protection will give you unlimited energy and provide you with insight into what is going on in your life.

The Hermetic Order of the Golden Dawn usually performed a shorter ritual called the Qabalistic Cross before performing the Lesser Banishing Ritual of the Pentagram. After visualizing the circle filling with white light, they helped the process by reaching skyward with their right hand and symbolically pulling the white light down. They continued the movement by making a sign of the cross on their bodies by touching their forehead, navel, and each side of their chest while saying "For thine" (while touching forehead), "is the kingdom" (while touching stomach), "the power" (touching right side of chest), "and the glory" (touching left side of chest). They continue by holding both hands over their heart while saying "forever. Amen." They finish this part of the ritual by extending their arms on each side to simulate a cross. I almost always perform the Qabalistic cross as I find it instantly puts me into the desired spiritual state of mind. You might like to experiment with this and use it, if you find it helpful (Regardie, 56–57).

You'll find the circle of protection extremely useful whenever you're working with the angelic realms. You can perform any ritual you wish while inside the circle, knowing that you're completely protected by Archangels Raphael, Michael, Gabriel, and Uriel. You might, for instance, say your prayers inside the circle and turn them into a ritual that strengthens your connection with the Divine.

GRATITUDE RITUAL WITH ARCHANGEL GABRIEL

This gratitude ritual is a good example of the type of ritual you can perform while inside the circle of protection. Being grateful for what you do have, rather than focusing on what you don't, helps you to focus on all of the positive aspects of your life. It also helps you develop spiritually.

It's easy to express gratitude when life is going well. It's much harder to do this when life is a struggle and nothing seems to work the way you want it to. In fact, most people become angry and upset when life isn't going the way they want it to and totally miss the spiritual lessons that are present in every experience. Very few people are able to accept the negative experiences as an opportunity to grow inwardly. Archangel Gabriel is responsible for gratitude (see the appendix). This is why we use him in this particular ritual. You'll find this a useful ritual to perform when life isn't going the way you'd like it to. However, with a few modifications, it can be changed to enable you to express gratitude at any time.

1. Create a circle of protection.

2. Sit down comfortably, close your eyes, and take several slow, deep breaths.

3. Think of something recent that involved you and was positive. It doesn't have to be anything life-changing—it might be as simple as someone smiling at you when you passed on the street. It might be coffee or a meal with a good friend. Relive the experience in your mind and express your gratitude to the universal life force for enabling it to happen.

4. Think of a person or animal you love. Remember some of the happy times you spent together. Again, express

your thanks to the universal life force for bringing you together.

5. Think of a time when you were honored or appreciated by others. This doesn't have to be anything of major significance—a childhood birthday party would be fine. Relive this special event and express your thanks to the universal life force for the fact that it happened.

6. Think about what's going on in your life at the moment. If life isn't easy right now, accept that what's happened has happened, and there's nothing you can do about it. You can become angry and upset, but that will do nothing to make the situation go away. Tell yourself that you've survived difficult situations in the past and that the problems were ultimately resolved and your life returned to normal. This problem will soon be behind you, too.

7. Turn to face Archangel Gabriel. Open your eyes, and speak to him. You might say: "Thank you, Archangel Gabriel, for all the blessings in my life. I'm deeply grateful to you for helping me whenever I've needed it. Right now, I need to turn this experience to the highest good. I want to grow spiritually as a result of what's happened. Please help me achieve this. I need your help."

8. Close your eyes and sit quietly for a couple of minutes. Focus on your breathing and wait to see what insights or thoughts Archangel Gabriel gives you. Spend a couple of minutes in silence after Gabriel has finished communicating with you, just in case he has more information for you at this time.

9. When you feel ready, finish the ritual by thanking Archangel Gabriel for his help. Express your gratitude to him for everything he's done.

10. Close the circle of protection.

11. Silently count from one to five, open your eyes, stretch, and stand up.

12. As soon as possible, once the ritual is over, ground yourself by eating a few nuts and raisins, and drinking a glass of water.

HEALING RITUAL WITH ARCHANGEL RAPHAEL

Nothing is more important to our well-being than good health. Raphael, the archangel of healing, wants you to enjoy vibrant health spiritually, emotionally, mentally, and physically. Most of the time, Raphael and the other healing angels will gently encourage you to do whatever is necessary when you need healing. If it's something minor, the angels will help you find the appropriate remedy, and you'll be able to carry on with your life without even knowing that healing angels had intervened to help you.

Many years ago, a friend of mine experienced a burning sensation in his abdomen and thought he had a stomach ulcer. He made an appointment to see his regular doctor, but cancelled it and went to see another doctor instead shortly before the appointment. When I asked him about the last-minute switch, he couldn't explain why he'd done it but felt that the new doctor "seemed right" for his concern. No one had recommended the other doctor to him, but he turned out to be an expert in duodenal medicine, and the problem was quickly resolved. I think it's possible that an angel quietly intervened and encouraged my friend to visit a doctor who was a specialist in his particular problem.

Angels are beings of light. They are made from God's life energy and use light, color, and vibration to provide healing at every level. We, in turn, possess auras that are electromagnetic fields made up of light, color, and vibration. Because of this, the healing angels possess the exact same energy that we do and are able to use it to heal our auric fields.

Your aura contains all the colors of the rainbow. Its size and appearance is determined by a number of factors, including your health. Someone who is kind, generous, and empathetic will have a large aura, and the colors will glow with life and energy. Someone who is dishonest and deceitful will have a smaller aura with murky colors. Jesus may have been referring to auras when he said: "Let your light so shine before men, that they may see your good works" (Matthew 5:16).

You can perform the following ritual any time you wish. It will cleanse your aura, fill you with energy, and enable you to strengthen your connection with Archangel Raphael.

1. Create a circle of protection.

2. Sit down, close your eyes, and take several slow, deep breaths. Allow your body to relax as much as possible each time you exhale. I find it helpful to say to myself, "relax, relax, relax" as I do this.

3. When you feel completely relaxed, ask Archangel Raphael to join you. Once you feel his presence, visualize yourself outdoors in a beautiful rural setting. You and Raphael are standing at the foot of a beautiful rainbow. It's a beautiful semicircle of vibrant colors that towers high above you and curves and descends into a valley several hundred yards away. The colors are indescribably vivid, and you feel incredibly fortunate and

privileged to be able to see a rainbow so close to you that you could reach out and touch it.

4. You gaze at the beautiful sight for what seems like a long time, and then Raphael takes you by the hand and leads you into the rainbow. You stop once you're completely surrounded by the stimulating and vibrant red color. As you breathe in the red energy, you feel your whole being filling up with energy and vitality. Take several deep breaths of the beautiful, energizing red color.

5. Raphael senses when you feel ready to start moving forward again. You keep walking until you're completely surrounded by the breathtaking orange energy. Sense a profound sense of peace and tranquility as you stand inside a world of orange. Take as many deep breaths of orange energy as you wish, and feel it reach every part of your body.

6. Raphael leads you on to the yellow area of the rainbow. You'll immediately experience the tremendous joy and happiness it gives to every cell of your body. You're likely to feel mentally stimulated, as well. Take deep breaths of yellow energy and enjoy the pleasure and sense of fun it gives to every part of your being.

7. Raphael tells you there's no need to hurry, and you can stay inside the yellow for as long as you want. He instinctively knows when the time is right to lead you on to the green section of the aura. You'll sense the healing power of green before you start inhaling deep breaths of green energy. It's a powerful, loving color, and you may feel a sense of oneness with all of God's

creation as you're completely surrounded by the peace and love of green energy.

8. Raphael laughs as you experience a sudden sense of enthusiasm and excitement as you move into the blue section of the rainbow. You may feel younger, and you'll certainly feel energetic and ready for anything as you take in deep breaths of blue energy.

9. The changes are more subtle as Raphael leads you into the indigo and you start experiencing the energy of its rays. You'll sense your intuition and the power of your hunches and feelings. You'll feel a strong connection with your home, family, and all the people you love as you take in deep breaths of pure indigo energy.

10. Raphael encourages you to lead the way into the violet sector. You'll know why violet has always been considered a spiritual color the moment you step into the violet section and experience its energy. You'll experience an overwhelming sensation of peace and love, and realize that you're in the presence of the Divine.

11. You enjoy the healing rays of violet for as long as you wish, and then you and Raphael walk out of the aura and back into the beautiful countryside you were in before you started walking through the rainbow.

12. You and Raphael walk over to a bench and sit down together. From this position you can see the entire rainbow. You ask Raphael to scan your aura to make sure that you've received the maximum benefit from each color of the rainbow. Most of the time, he'll tell you that your aura is looking magnificent after your walk through the rainbow. If any of the colors are depleted,

he'll ask you mentally return to them in the rainbow, and take as many deep breaths as necessary, until every color in your aura is glowing.

13. When you feel ready, thank Raphael for his help and company, and say goodbye. Count slowly from one to five, and open your eyes.

14. Close the circle of protection, have something to eat and drink, and carry on with your day.

This is a powerful ritual that leaves you deeply healed and revitalized in mind, body, and spirit. It activates every cell in your body, releasing negativity while enhancing positivity.

I enjoy performing this ritual, but it takes twenty to thirty minutes depending on the amount of time spent inhaling the different colors. If you're short on time, you can do an abbreviated version of this ritual, which takes only two or three minutes to perform. Sit or lie down somewhere comfortable. Close your eyes, and take several deep breaths to help you relax. Imagine that you're surrounded with pure red energy. Take a deep breath of red, and allow it to fill your body with all the energy that this color provides. Continue doing this with all the other colors of the rainbow. Once you've done this, ask Archangel Raphael to join you. When you sense his presence, ask him to look at your aura. He may suggest you take a few more deep breaths of one or more colors. Once he's happy with the way your aura looks, thank him for his help and say goodbye. Silently count from one to five and open your eyes. You can also do this if you need more of a certain color's energy. If you need more enthusiasm and energy, for instance, you can simply close your eyes and take in three or four large breaths of red energy. If you need healing, breathe in green.

FORGIVENESS RITUAL WITH ARCHANGEL ZADKIEL

It's vitally important to our health and well-being to forgive others and ourselves, but it's not always easy to do. Most people find it easy to forget minor hurts, but it can be a different matter if the pain was caused deliberately and maliciously, maybe even by someone considered close. Sometimes it's not possible to walk away, either, especially if the pain has been caused even unintentionally by a parent, sibling, or partner. Sometimes minor hurts can be blown up out of proportion and ultimately cause damage to the body, heart, mind, and soul of the person who is holding onto it.

Forgiveness helps you. When you forgive someone for whatever they did to upset you, you automatically forgive yourself at the same time. Holding onto a grudge makes you a victim. Forgiving the perpetrator allows you to let go of the resentment and pain and start healing yourself. It gives you your power back and enables you to put all the wasted time you spent dwelling on the situation to better use. You'll become a more positive, confident, and stronger person.

Forgiveness also makes you more compassionate and understanding. This ritual with Archangel Zadkiel will help you forgive yourself and others, and develop spiritually in the process.

Before you perform the ritual, you need to write a letter to the person who hurt you. As this person won't read it, you can say anything you wish. You might start out by saying how the person made you feel when they did whatever it was. Follow this by saying that you are choosing to forgive them and also yourself for whatever role you played in what happened to cause the distress. Finish by saying the matter is now in the past. You might not forget it, but you are now free and will start moving forward in life. Wish the other person happiness and success in the future, and sign the letter using the word "love."

Put the letter aside for at least twenty-four hours before performing the ritual. This is because you might want to make a few changes or perhaps add or delete something. Once you're happy that you've written everything you wish to say, seal the letter in an envelope and write the person's name on the front.

Required:

- A table
- 1 violet (or white) candle
- A teaspoon of earth
- A glass of water
- A large bowl (to burn the letter in)
- The forgiveness letter

Preparation:

1. Place a table in the center of the area you'll construct the circle of protection around. Place the candle in the center of the table, and put the bowl immediately behind it. Place the letter on the left-hand side of table, and the earth and water on the right-hand side.

2. Have a shower or bath, and dress in fresh, loose-fitting clothes.

Ritual:

1. Stand in front of the table and create the circle of protection.

2. Light the candle.

3. Turn to face east and ask Archangel Zadkiel to join you. You might want to close your eyes until you sense his presence.

4. Thank Zadkiel for coming to your aid. Tell him exactly what happened and how you felt about it. Tell him that the time has come to let the matter go, and that you're forgiving the other person unconditionally.

5. Ask Archangel Zadkiel to help you forgive the person who caused you so much pain. Lower your head and close your eyes until you feel Zadkiel's healing energy coursing through your body. Open your eyes and thank Zadkiel for his help.

6. Ask Archangel Zadkiel to help you forgive yourself. Lower your head and close your eyes until you sense Zadkiel's healing energy once more. Open your eyes and thank him for his help.

7. Ask Archangel Zadkiel if he would help you perform a small ritual to heal your body, mind, and spirit.

8. Turn to face the altar and pick up the letter. Show it to Archangel Zadkiel. If you wish, you can open it and read the letter to Zadkiel.

9. Turn to face Archangel Raphael. Thank him for all his healing work and for restoring wholeness to your life. Ask him if you can use the element of air in the ritual. Wait until you sense his agreement, and then pass the letter through the smoke coming from the candle.

10. Turn to face Archangel Michael. Thank him for providing you with courage and for helping you become the person you really are. Ask him if you can use the element of fire in the ritual. After you sense his agreement,

indicate the candle, and say that you want to use it to complete the elemental ritual.

11. Turn to face Archangel Gabriel. Thank her for her purification and guidance. Ask her if you can use the element of water in the ritual. Wait until you sense her agreement, then dip your fingers into the glass of water and sprinkle a few drops onto the envelope.

12. Turn to face Archangel Uriel. Thank him for providing you with peace of mind and for releasing your fears. Ask him if you can use the element of earth in the ritual. Wait until you sense his agreement and then sprinkle a few grains of earth onto the envelope.

13. Turn to Archangel Zadkiel and tell him that you have the blessing of the four great archangels to proceed with the ritual, and that you'd now like to use the element of fire to send the letter out into the universe.

14. Turn to face Archangel Raphael, and bow slightly as you thank him for his help. Face Michael, Gabriel, and Uriel in turn and thank them.

15. Turn back to Archangel Zadkiel and tell him that with his help and with the help and love of the four great archangels, you are ready to forgive the person unconditionally and allow the matter to be forgotten. Repeat your reasons for performing the ritual. These might include: putting the past behind you, ceasing to be a victim, enjoying better health, eliminating negativity, and healing yourself.

16. Hold the envelope high in the air for a few moments, and then hold it in the flame of the candle. Once it is burning, drop it into the bowl, and watch the smoke rise

upward and out into the universe. Say, "I forgive (person's name) unconditionally, and I also forgive myself." Continue saying this until the envelope is completely burned.

17. When the fire goes out, inhale deeply, spread your arms out wide, and gaze heavenward. Allow yourself to enjoy the sense of freedom and happiness you've gained as a result of forgiving yourself and the other person.

18. When you feel ready, snuff out the candle. Turn to Archangel Zadkiel and thank him for all his help. Tell him exactly how you feel and how positive your future is going to be now that you're free of the pain and suffering that the hurt created. Thank Zadkiel again, and say goodbye. You may feel a gentle touch or even a hug as Zadkiel responds to your words and leaves.

19. Close the circle of protection by thanking Raphael, Uriel, Gabriel, and Michael in turn.

20. Relax for a minute or two, and then have something to eat and drink before carrying on with your day.

PEACE OF MIND RITUAL WITH ARCHANGEL URIEL

Everyday life is full of minor inconveniences and hassles. If you add negative people, grudges, and impatience to the mix, you're bound to feel stressed and worried. It's hard to experience mental and emotional peace in the midst of all the hustle and bustle of everyday life.

Fortunately, there are many ways to find peace of mind. Listening to music, meditating, going for a walk, enjoying nature, reading a book, and laughing are all good ways to find peace of mind. Mindfulness has become extremely popular in recent years. It's a technique that enables you to live entirely in the present moment and be totally aware of your senses of touch, taste, sight, hearing, and smell. As we're all unique individuals, what works for you may not work for someone else. I love walking, for instance, but I know many people who won't walk anywhere as they gain no pleasure at all from this gentle form of exercise.

Think of the activities that give you most pleasure. It might be spending time with someone you love. It could be watching a favorite movie or TV program. It might be dinner at a nice restaurant with some close friends. It might be sitting on a beach. Whatever your favorite activities are will tell you when you're living in the moment and experiencing peace of mind.

Of course, none of us can spend all our time enjoying pleasurable activities, and sooner or later we have to return to our everyday lives. Fortunately, Archangel Uriel will help you attain peace of mind, and retain it long after the ritual is over. Of course, you can repeat the ritual whenever you need to regain your inner peace.

1. Change into loose-fitting comfortable clothes, and find a quiet place where you will not be disturbed for at least thirty minutes. I like to perform this outdoors whenever possible, but it depends on the weather and the season. If you're doing this indoors, make sure the room is pleasantly warm. You might like to cover yourself with a blanket. Sit down in a comfortable chair and relax.

2. Close your eyes and take several slow, deep breaths. Focus on your breathing, and say silently "relax, relax, relax" with each exhalation. Once you feel pleasantly relaxed, forget about your breathing and focus on the

different muscles in your body, starting with your feet. When they feel relaxed, focus on your calf muscles, and gradually work your way up your body to the top of your head. Once you feel totally relaxed, mentally scan your body to see if there are any areas of tension remaining. Relax these, and then scan yourself again to ensure that you're totally relaxed.

3. Take another deep breath, and exhale slowly. In your mind, picture yourself sitting in a beautiful garden. It's dusk, and you're watching the night fall, while enjoying the pleasant scent of the beautiful flowers that are all around you. It's pleasantly warm, and you feel peaceful and relaxed. You watch the sun slowly disappear over the horizon. Suddenly, it's dark, and you notice a large hand in front of you, palm facing up. It surprises you that you haven't noticed it before, as it is huge. The reason you can see it at all is because there's a flame burning on the palm of this hand. As the hand is held steady, you realize that the hand is experiencing no pain. You know that this flame is the symbol of Uriel, and that the flame is the fire of love. You gaze at the flame and watch it flicker and dance. This is Uriel's gift to humanity, a flame of love that can provide you with emotional healing and peace of mind whenever you need it.

4. As you gaze at the flame, you become aware that Uriel is there with you, and that the flame is burning in the palm of his hand. You feel a sense of excitement as you realize that you can ask Uriel anything you wish. You feel totally relaxed, even though you know that you're sitting in a garden with an archangel. It feels per-

fectly natural and normal to be sitting with Archangel Uriel. You feel more at peace than you have ever been before, and this is because you know that you're surrounded and enfolded by Uriel's love and compassion. You know that he'll listen sympathetically and will do everything he can to help you.

5. Tell Uriel everything that's on your mind. Tell him about your concerns and problems, and explain why you need to regain your peace of mind. Ask him for advice on what you can do to take life as it comes, to live in the present, and to enjoy quiet moments of contentment. When you've finished talking, sit quietly for a minute or two and wait for Uriel's response. You may receive this as thoughts in your mind or perhaps be lucky enough to receive a verbal reply. You may sense that all is well, and life will go more smoothly now that Uriel has attended to your concerns.

6. Spend as long as you need with Uriel. He's famous for his patience and will be happy to spend as much time as necessary to help you resolve your problems. When you've finished, thank him sincerely for his love, support, and help. Smile, and enjoy Uriel's company for several seconds before saying goodbye. Once you've said goodbye, you'll notice Uriel's hand and the flame become fainter and fainter until they disappear from sight. Visualize yourself, in your mind's eye, relaxed in the beautiful garden. When you feel ready, return to the room you're in, become aware of your surroundings, and count to five slowly before opening your eyes.

7. Ground yourself by having something to eat and drink as soon as possible after the ritual has ended.

You're likely to feel exhilarated after spending time with Uriel. You'll feel positive about the future and have a sense of calmness and inner peace. Problems that seemed insurmountable before will now seem easy to overcome, and you'll have greater insight into the motivations of others.

Your connection with Uriel will increase each time you perform this meditation. With practice, you will reach a stage where you can sit down, take a few deep breaths, and instantly be in the garden conversing with Uriel. However, this meditation is not intended to be done quickly; I usually take several minutes to reach the garden, because I find the process incredibly peaceful and relaxing.

THREE CHAMUEL LOVE RITUALS

Archangel Chamuel is the angel of compassion and unconditional love. He can be called upon to help with any matters involving love. Consequently, he is frequently called upon to attract love, strengthen the bonds between two people who are in love with each other, and help mend a broken heart. Chamuel also helps people to heal themselves emotionally, to love themselves, and to accept others as they are.

Love Attraction Ritual

You can perform this ritual whenever you wish, but the best time is when the moon is waxing (growing), as this means you'll be working in harmony with nature's regular rhythms.

Before performing the ritual, spend a bit of time thinking about the person you'd like to meet. Write down the qualities this person will need to have. Your list might include: loving, kind, gentle, considerate, and strong. You should also include interests that the two of you will need to have in common, such as the same taste in music and movies. You might like to prepare this list over a few days, adding different qualities as they occur to you.

Prepare your room beforehand. Display some objects that remind you of love. These might include pictures of obviously happy couples, anything that's heart-shaped, red roses or other flowers, and pairs of anything that reminds you of love and romance. The room should be pleasantly warm. Enjoy a leisurely bath or shower before the ritual. Dress yourself in loose-fitting clothing that ideally makes you feel romantic. Use a small amount of a favorite perfume, or scent the room in some other way.

Required:

- A table to act as an altar
- A straight-backed chair
- 2 pink candles (use white or red candles, if you don't have any pink ones)

1. Place your altar in the center of the room, and set the candles on it about six inches apart. Place the chair about four feet away from the altar.

2. Create a circle of protection around you. It needs to be large enough to include the altar and chair.

3. Sit down in the chair facing the altar. Look at the two candles and think of your desire for the right partner. Read the list of attributes that your ideal partner will possess. Read it out loud, if possible. Naturally, if other people are nearby, you might have to read it silently.

4. Light the candle on your left side. As you do this, say something along the lines of: "This candle represents me. I'm sending my light and love out into the universe."

5. Light the other candle while saying: "This candle symbolizes the partner I've yet to meet. He/she is sending his/her light out into the universe."

6. Sit down again and gaze at the two candles. In your imagination, visualize them moving closer and closer together until they become one.

7. Close your eyes and ask Archangel Chamuel for his help. You might say: "Archangel Chamuel, please come to my aid. I've been on my own for too long, and my greatest wish is to find the right partner to share my life with. I have plenty of love to give, and I'm seeking someone who'll love me just as much as I'll love them. Please, Archangel Chamuel, come to me and help me find the right person. Thank you, Archangel Chamuel."

8. Open your eyes and gaze at the space between the two candles. Think about the partner you desire and the different qualities he/she will possess. You'll gradually become aware that Archangel Chamuel is with you. This will probably come as a feeling that he's beside you, though you may notice a change in the temperature of the room, or the candles may start flickering. You may feel yourself enfolded in his wings or even see a brief flash of swirling color, signifying Chamuel's presence.

9. Once you know he's with you, you can stop gazing at the candles. Start talking to Chamuel. Thank him for visiting you. Talk to him as if you were chatting with

a close and special friend. You'll probably do this auto-matically, as Chamuel is a warm, empathetic, and lov-ing angel who has your best interests at heart. Tell him about your experiences of love in the past, and how you desire the right person in your life. Tell him about your hopes for the future, and how the right partner would enrich your life in every way. Read him the list of quali-ties you'd written down, and ask him for his help.

10. When you've finished talking, sit quietly and wait for Chamuel's response. This response can come in a vari-ety of ways. You may experience a sense of knowing that Chamuel will start the process of helping you attract the right partner. His answer may come in the form of thoughts in your head. You'll know from their content that they've come from Chamuel. You may be fortunate enough to actually hear Chamuel's response. You're likely to experience this as if someone was whis-pering in your ear. You may experience nothing at all, which is common, and nothing to be concerned about. You may have missed the quiet response Chamuel gave you, or he may be mulling over what you told him. Know that you've told Chamuel what you want, and leave it in his hands.

11. Thank Chamuel for coming to your aid and listening to you. Thank him also for his help. Tell him that you'd love to talk with him again soon and say goodbye.

12. Gaze between the candles again and visualize them get-ting closer and closer together until they merge into one.

13. Stand up and snuff out the candles. The ritual is now over. I like to say a prayer at the end before closing the

circle; you may or may not choose to do the same. My prayer has nothing to do with my request to Chamuel—it's simply a prayer of thanks to the Divine for the gift of life and for all the blessings I enjoy in my life.

14. Close the circle by facing east and thanking Raphael for protecting you during the ritual. Thank Michael, Gabriel, and Uriel in turn.

15. Ground yourself by eating and drinking something before carrying on with your day.

You can perform this ritual as often as you wish until you've found the right person. Do it two or three times a week if you feel you have yet to receive a response from Chamuel. In time, you will. Repeat the ritual about once a week if you did receive a response. Remember that you don't necessarily need to perform the entire ritual every time. You can talk to Chamuel whenever you wish by creating a circle of joy or by speaking to him directly.

Love-Strengthening Ritual

This ritual is an effective way to communicate with Archangel Chamuel when you're inside a good relationship, and want it to become even closer. You can perform this ritual on your own, or with your partner. I'll describe it as if you're doing it on your own, and will discuss how to perform it together at the end.

Start by preparing your room. Display some pictures of you and your partner, in addition to anything else that reminds you of your lives together. Place a table and chair in position, and make sure the room is warm, inviting, and smells wonderful. Enjoy a leisurely bath or shower, and dress in comfortable clothes that are preferably romantic and make you feel good.

Required:

- A table to act as an altar
- A straight-backed chair
- 2 red candles. (Use pink or white candles if you don't have red ones)

1. Create a circle of protection.

2. Light the two candles. As you light the first one, say something along the lines of: "By lighting this candle, I'm sending all my love to (person's name)." As you light the second candle, say: "I'm lighting this candle to symbolize all the love that (person's name) is sending to me."

3. Sit down in the chair and gaze at the two candles. Smile as you think about the love they represent, and the joy and happiness that has come into your life since you and your partner met.

4. Close your eyes and ask Archangel Chamuel if he would join you to help make the special relationship you and your partner have even closer and better than it already is. Keep your eyes closed until you sense that Chamuel is with you.

5. Once Chamuel has arrived, open your eyes and thank Chamuel for joining you. Tell him about your relationship. Tell him about all the good things, such as how much you love each other, but also let him know about any niggles or difficulties you and your partner might be experiencing. No relationship is perfect all the time, and everyone has disagreements every now and again. Ask Chamuel to help the two of you develop the close

bond you already have, as you're committed to each other, and want the relationship to be the very best it can be. Ask Chamuel to surround you and your partner with his love.

6. Sit quietly for a minute or two and watch the flickering flames of the candles. Gradually, thoughts and ideas will come into your mind. This will be Chamuel giving you advice on what you can do to enhance your relationship. Obviously the advice will be different for everyone, but he might, for instance, suggest you compliment each other more frequently, or that you would benefit from scheduling regular date nights. He might even give advice on how to resolve any conflicts more effectively.

7. When Chamuel finishes, thank him sincerely for his advice. Ask questions about anything you don't fully understand. Once you've learned everything you need to know, thank Chamuel again and ask him if he'd mind if you called for him every now and again when you need more advice. Say goodbye, and notice the different feeling in the room as soon as he's left.

8. If you wish, say a prayer of thanks to the Divine. Snuff out the candles and close the circle by thanking the four archangels in turn.

9. Eat and drink something before carrying on with your day.

The ritual described above is intended to enhance the quality of a relationship. Consequently, one would assume that it would be more effective if both people were involved. Although it would ideally, your partner must be as interested as you are in the angelic realms for it to work well. If your partner is not particularly interested in angels, you'll have better results performing on your own.

If your partner is interested, the ritual itself will help you become closer. Naturally, you'll need two chairs rather than one, and you'll light one candle each. You'll both be able to communicate with Archangel Chamuel. I've found that it works well if one person creates the circle of protection and the other closes it. However, as not everyone I've spoken to about this agrees, it is best to experiment and make up your own mind.

How to Mend a Broken Heart

Healing a broken heart takes time and effort. The pain and trauma can be devastating and affect you physically as well as emotionally. You'll experience periods of disbelief, denial, anger, and heartache. Consequently, it's vital to take good care of yourself. It's important to let your feelings out, and you should grieve in whatever way you wish. Some people prefer to grieve on their own, while others prefer the support of people who are close to them. Even if you'd rather grieve on your own, by yourself, in your own way, don't isolate yourself from the people who love you. You may not want to discuss all the details of what's happened with them, but you still need their love and support. Some people record their thoughts and feelings in a journal, while others punch a pillow, cry, or talk about their feelings with others.

Above all, always be kind to yourself. Eat good food, drink plenty of water, and engage in some form of exercise, preferably an activity that takes you outdoors, such as walking. Nurture yourself by finding something enjoyable to do every day, such as spending time with a good friend, having a massage, watching a comedy on television, or reading a good book. The process of mending a broken heart is different for everyone. Give yourself whatever time and space you need to heal. Don't hesitate to get professional help if it seems impossible to overcome the grief on your own.

Call on Chamuel for help whenever you wish. Simply start talking to him, silently or out loud, wherever you happen to be, and listen carefully for his responses. He'll provide comfort, support, healing, and love. When he feels the time is right, he'll offer advice and suggestions on what you can do to ease the pain and start living again. He'll help you understand that the relationship is over, and that you need to forgive yourself and your former partner, so you can move forward again.

This ritual will help you mend your broken heart but shouldn't be done until you've gone through at least part of the grieving process.

Required:

- A table to act as an altar
- A chair
- Two or three sheets of good-quality writing paper
- An envelope
- A pen
- A pebble or small stone. Ideally, this stone should be about an inch in diameter, and one that you picked up from a place that has many similar stones.
- A pink candle
- A ceramic or metal bowl

1. Create a circle of protection.

2. Light the candle and place it in the center of your altar. While doing this, say: "I am deserving of love. I deserve the best that the world has to offer."

3. Sit down in front of the altar. Pick up the pen and write a goodbye letter to the person who broke your heart. Mention some of the good times the two of you had together before everything went wrong. Tell this person how the breakup made you feel, and describe the anger, hurt, disbelief, and emotional ups and downs you have experienced since you broke up. Tell them that you are much stronger now, that you're on the road to recovery, and you're letting them go. Write that you have forgiven them and yourself for everything that has happened and that you now consider it to be a learning experience, one that will make you a better person and a better partner in the future. Finish by wishing this person success and happiness in the future, and sign your name.

4. Pick up the candle and gaze into its flames. Tell yourself that you are a very special, lovable person and that you will never settle for second best. Your time with (former partner's name) was necessary for your growth, but it's over and done with. You're letting it go. Place the candle back onto the altar.

5. Pick up the stone and hold it in the palm of your non-dominant hand (e.g., your left hand if you're right-handed). Gently caress it with the fingers of your other hand and thank it for participating in your ritual. Place it back on the altar.

6. Pick up the letter you wrote and read it, out loud if possible. While doing this, think of any changes you'd like to make to the letter. You might want add something or make some alterations to what you wrote. Once you're satisfied that you've said everything you want to say, place the letter into the envelope, seal it, and write your former partner's first name on the front. Place the stone on top of it.

7. Close your eyes and ask Archangel Chamuel to join you. Once you sense that he is with you, thank him for coming to your aid today and express your gratitude for all of the help he has provided in enabling you to get over your heartbreak. Tell him honestly exactly how you feel about performing this ritual and how you hope to feel once it's completed. You may have worries and concerns about loneliness, and the thought of being on your own might be frightening. Ask Chamuel for his suggestions on what you should do in the coming days, weeks, and months. Continue asking Chamuel as many questions as you wish. When the conversation is over, ask him to stay with you, as you have something important to do once you've completed the ritual.

8. Open your eyes. Place the stone to one side, and pick up the letter. Speak to the person you're going to send it to. Tell them that they no longer exist, as far as you're concerned. If you ever meet again, you'll exchange a few pleasantries and move on. All emotional attachments have completely gone. Say goodbye, and set fire to the letter. Once it's alight, place it in the bowl and watch the smoke rise up and dissipate out into the uni-

verse. Take a few slow, deep breaths, and say goodbye with each exhalation.

9. Wait until the flame has burned out. Close your eyes and say a prayer to the universal life force, expressing your gratitude for the gift of life, for all the gifts you have, and for the opportunities you have to do good in this lifetime.

10. When you feel ready, snuff out the candle. Close the circle by thanking and dismissing the four archangels in turn.

The main part of the ritual is over. However, there's still something important you need to do with the stone. Before doing it, though, have something to eat and drink to help ground you again. I eat nuts and raisins and drink a glass of water.

Once this stage is over and as soon as possible, return to the place where you picked up the stone. Caress it as you did before, and thank it for helping you perform the ritual. Hold the stone in your dominant hand and start walking away. After you've taken several steps, toss the stone over your shoulder while saying goodbye. Don't look back to see where it landed. The stone symbolizes the relationship that is now totally left in the past. You can now walk with a spring in your step, head held high as your life is beginning again.

After walking for a minute or two, thank Archangel Chamuel for helping you restore your broken heart. "I'm fine now," you might say. "I'm ready to start again. I'm so grateful to you for all your help. I might need more advice and love before I'm totally healed, and I'm so happy that you're willing to help me every step of the way. I love you, Archangel Chamuel. Thank you so very much for everything." Pause and wait to hear what Chamuel has to say. You might have another conversation, or he might simply say "You're welcome," or "Goodbye." You might feel a gentle touch or be lucky enough to experience a hug before he leaves. Once he's gone, the ritual is finally over.

You might have to perform this ritual a number of times before you feel totally free and confident about moving forward in your life. This doesn't matter, as you'll feel better and better about yourself each time you perform it.

JOPHIEL WISDOM RITUAL

Jophiel provides joy and happiness everywhere he goes. He loves beauty and wants people to slow down long enough to appreciate all the beauty in the world. He enjoys working with people who create beauty, such as artists and people who create beauty by the way they live their lives. Jophiel also provides mental clarity and helps people release problems caused by their negative thoughts, feelings, and emotions.

Required:

- A straight-backed chair
- A table
- A yellow candle (use a white candle if you don't have a yellow one)
- Several photographs or illustrations of beautiful scenes

If possible, start this ritual by spending time in beautiful surroundings. You might like to walk in a park, sit in your favorite place in your home or garden, or maybe walk along a beach. It doesn't matter where the setting is as long as you find it peaceful and attractive. Appreciate the beauty of your surroundings and keep your thoughts as positive as possible.

Follow this with a pleasant shower or bath. Change into clean, comfortable, loose-fitting clothes.

Place the candle and the images on the altar.

1. Create a circle of protection.

2. Sit in the chair and look at the pictures, one at a time. Notice something specific that you like in each one before moving on to the next one. When you've looked at them all, silently thank Archangel Jophiel for everything he does to beautify the world. Place the illustrations down on the table.

3. Light the candle. As you do, speak to Archangel Jophiel. You might say: "I know you like all the colors of the rainbow, Archangel Jophiel, but I understand that you like yellow more than any other. I'm lighting this candle to thank you for everything you've done for me, and to welcome you into my special angelic circle."

4. Close your eyes and say a prayer. You might like to start with a favorite prayer, such as the Lord's Prayer, and then thank the Divine for all the blessings you have in your life. Say a sincere "amen" at the end.

5. Visualize a beautiful stream of yellow energy flowing down from the heavens and entering your body through the top of your head. It gradually fills up every cell of your body, and then with each exhalation, flows out to fill your circle of protection with divine love. You feel a sense of happiness, joy, and incredible love.

6. Sit quietly and think of Archangel Jophiel. Think of the illustrations you were looking at, and thank Jophiel for his energy and efforts to maintain and enhance such a

beautiful world. Thank him for his special gift of joy and laughter, and let him know how much you appreciate all the happiness he brings into your life. Thank him also for his clarity and wisdom.

7. Remain sitting quietly, eyes closed, and ask Archangel Jophiel to join you. Wait patiently until you're sure he's with you. You might sense his presence, notice a slight change in the energy of the room you're in, or possibly see him in your mind's eye. You might even hear a slight movement as he enters the circle.

8. When you feel Jophiel's presence, thank him for joining you. Tell him how much you appreciate everything he does, and then ask him for help. Tell him exactly what you need in your life right now. You might, for instance, need help to resolve a particular problem. You might be feeling weighed down and despondent and need more joy in your life. You might need Jophiel's help to "beautify" your thoughts and make them more positive than they currently are. It doesn't matter what your concern may be. Jophiel will listen to everything you have to say. When you've finished, thank him for listening, and wait quietly for his reply. It may come as a feeling that everything will be all right and the matter will be resolved. Jophiel might talk to you in the form of thoughts and ideas inside your head. You might even hear him speaking to you. Answer anything he asks, and continue conversing with him until you have all the ideas and answers you need.

9. When you've finished, thank him for his care, love, and advice, and say goodbye.

10. Say another prayer to the Divine, giving thanks for the precious gift of life and for all the love and blessings you have in your life. Give thanks also for the presence of the angels and the help and support they give to you. When you've finished your prayer, say "Amen."

11. Silently count from one to five and open your eyes. Familiarize yourself with your surroundings, and then snuff out the candle while saying, "Thank you, Archangel Jophiel."

12. Close the circle of protection, and carry on with your day after grounding yourself with something to eat and drink.

You can repeat this ritual as often as you wish. You'll find the illustrations will have gained energy from the ritual, too, and you can look at them whenever you feel the need for instant beauty and positivity in your life.

MICHAEL PROTECTION RITUAL

Michael can be called upon for protection at any time. You don't need to perform a ritual if your need is desperate or urgent. All you need do is call out to Michael, ideally out loud, saying, "Archangel Michael, I need your help now!" Michael will instantly recognize your situation and come to your aid. I've needed to do this a few times over the years, and each time Michael was with me by the time I'd finished calling on him.

If the need isn't urgent or you want to speak to Michael for some other purpose, such as helping you find the truth about something, or maybe providing you with the energy and strength you need, you can perform this simple ritual at any time.

1. Sit down quietly somewhere where you won't be disturbed, close your eyes, and take ten slow deep breaths. Each time you exhale, say to yourself: "Relax, relax, relax."

2. Forget about your breathing. Mentally scan your body to make sure that you're completely relaxed. Focus on any areas that are still tense until they let go and relax.

3. Speak to Archangel Michael. Thank him for looking after you and for interceding whenever you needed help. Tell him what's going on in your life, and then ask him to protect your body and aura.

4. Visualize Archangel Michael surrounding you with love. In your mind, see him holding a hand, palm facing down over your head. As you watch, a brilliant, pure, deep blue light flows from his palm and surrounds you with an intense feeling of love and joy. You feel safe and protected.

5. Thank Archangel Michael for providing you with all the protection you need to handle any situation that might occur. When you feel ready, thank Michael again and say goodbye.

6. Spend a minute or two enjoying the stimulation and energy that Michael has filled you with.

7. When you feel ready, open your eyes and carry on with your day.

8. As often as possible during the day, affirm to yourself that Michael has surrounded you with divine protection and that you can accomplish anything.

If you need Michael to protect you for a specific reason, you can perform a full Archangel Michael Protection Ritual. You can perform this ritual whenever you wish, but the best time is when the moon is full or waxing in size.

Required:

- A table to act as an altar
- A chair
- A blue, purple or gold candle
- A saucer
- Pen and paper
- Two or three protective herbs (fresh or dried). Choose from basil, blueberry, cumin, dill, lavender, marjoram, oregano, or parsley
- A teaspoon of salt

Preparation:

Set up your altar ahead of time. Place the candle in the center of the altar with the pen and paper in front of it and the saucer on its right side. Place a small container of salt on the left-hand side of the altar, and the herbs on the right. If you wish, you can display a picture of Archangel Michael, and maybe have a vase of blue or violet flowers on the altar as well. Place a container of water close by, just in case you need it. (You should always do this when working with fire.)

If possible, have a bath or shower before the ritual, and change into fresh, loose-fitting clothes.

1. Stand in front of your altar and create the circle of protection.

2. Light the candle. Follow this by picking up the salt container and sprinkling a few grains of salt around the circle of protection, starting in the east.

3. Sit down on the chair and think of your need for protection. Pick up the pen and write a letter to Archangel Michael. Start with "Dear Archangel Michael," and
   then write down exactly what you need to be protected
   against. Be as specific as you can. You might want protection from a person, a situation, or even the ill effects
   of stress and anxiety. Finish the letter by asking Michael
   to help you resolve the situation. When the letter is finished, sign it with your full name.

4. Stand up, and face Michael in the south. Tell Michael
   how grateful you are for his guidance, strength, and
   protection. Pick up the letter you have just written and
   read it out loud. Tell Michael anything you might wish
   to add, and then turn back to the altar. Place the letter
   on the altar again and sprinkle it with the herbs.

5. Face south again, and say a prayer to Michael. You can
   find many suitable prayers on the Internet, or you might
   prefer to create your own. One I like to use is the Prayer
   to St. Michael, written by Pope Leo XIII in 1886:

Saint Michael the Archangel,
Defend us in battle,
Be our protection against the wickedness
and snares of the devil;
May God rebuke him, we humbly pray;
And do thou, O Prince of the heavenly host,
By the power of God, thrust into hell

Satan and all evil spirits

Who prowl through the world seeking the ruin of souls.

Amen.

6. Turn back to your altar. Fold your letter into quarters, herbs and all. Face Michael in the south, and raise the letter as high as you can using both hands. Say, "Thank you, Archangel Michael. Thank you. Thank you. Thank you."

7. Turn back to the altar and burn the letter in the flame of the candle. Place the flaming letter into the saucer and watch it burn until nothing remains except the ashes.

8. Face south, and bow your head to Michael. Say one last, sincere "thank you." Close the circle.

As always, after performing a ritual, have something to eat and drink. To ground yourself, think about the ritual you've just experienced, and return once more to your everyday life.

ARCHANGELS OF THE ELEMENTS

The four elements of fire, earth, air, and water have been used for thousands of years to symbolize the fundamental building blocks of the universe. The Greek philosopher Empedocles of Acragas (ca. 494 BCE–ca. 434 BCE) is said to have discovered the four elements about twenty-five hundred years ago (Greer, 151). The concept of four elements was later popularized by Plato and Aristotle. One story about where this concept came from says that the elements described the only ways a dead body could be returned to where it came from: burning it with fire, burying it in the earth, given to the birds of the air, or thrown into water.

The elements are all essential to human life and have positive and negative aspects. Imagine what the earth would be like without air to surround it, water to wet and nourish it, or fire to warm it. This is an example of how the elements work together to create and sustain life.

AIR
Archangel: Raphael
Direction: East

Air surrounds us and is the lightest of the four elements. Air is essential for our survival, but can also be dangerous. It's wonderful when we sense it as a cooling breeze on a hot day, but it can be destructive when it appears in the form of a hurricane or tornado. Air is usually associated with the clouds, sky, winds, and birds.

This element is associated with thought and the intellect. This is why deep thinkers are sometimes described as "having their heads in the clouds." "Airheads" live more in their imaginations than they do in the real world. As he is associated with this element, Archangel Raphael provides spiritual, mental, emotional, and physical healing.

FIRE

Archangel: Michael
Direction: South

Fire symbolizes passion and energy. It can create and destroy. It's useful when it warms our homes or cooks a meal, but it can be extremely dangerous when it gets out of control. Fire is transformative, as it burns away the old to make room for something new and different. Many idioms illustrate the power of this element. Someone who is exhausted experiences burnout. People can become red (fire) with rage, or burn with lust. If you're unexpectedly put into a difficult situation, you might experience "a baptism by fire." You can "get out of the frying pan and into the fire." You might "light a fire" under someone who isn't motivated to act. As Archangel Michael is associated with fire, call on him to provide courage and protection.

WATER
Archangel: Gabriel
Direction: West

Water gives us life. Life as we know it evolved from the sea. Water is a blessing when it cleanses us, restores us when we're dehydrated, and rains gently onto gardens and fields. However, water can also be dangerous—floods and tsunamis have claimed the lives of countless millions of people. As Archangel Gabriel is associated with water, look to her for love, wisdom, and spiritual growth.

EARTH
Archangel: Uriel
Direction: North

Earth is the most stable of the four elements. It's often represented in rituals by stones, crystals, or salt. Earth is often used to cleanse ritual tools by burying them in the soil. People often stand barefooted on the ground to remove excess energy after performing a ritual. This is called grounding. Earth provides stability and prosperity. Archangel Uriel is associated with this element and can provide you understanding and inner peace.

As archangels look after the four elements, it's not surprising that certain archangels also look after the twelve signs of the zodiac, the months of the year, the days of the week, and even the hours of the day. We'll look at them in the next chapter.

ARCHANGELS OF THE ZODIAC

A ngels have been associated with the twelve signs of the zodiac for thousands of years. According to Jewish legend, Masleh is the angel in charge of the zodiac in addition to the four classical elements.

The angels of the zodiac are usually called upon by people seeking the qualities relating to a specific horoscope sign. You can call upon the archangel who rules your sign whenever you wish. If you're making a request for someone else, you should petition the angel that relates to his or her zodiac sign. You can call on any of the zodiacal archangels whenever necessary, but the best time is said to be on your birthday.

The German physician, theologian, and abbot, Johannes Trithemius (1462–1516), had two gifted students: Cornelius Agrippa (1486–1535), who became a celebrated occultist and writer, and Paracelsus (1493–1541), who became an astrologer, alchemist, and physician. Johannes Trithemius recorded a list of the "Angelic Governors of the Twelve Signs of the Zodiac" in his *Book of Secret Things* (ca. 1500). Medieval magicians called on the archangels of the zodiac for many purposes and created a large number of lists. In his *Three Books of Occult Philosophy*, Cornelius Agrippa mentioned twelve other angels who are frequently associated with the different signs of the zodiac (Agrippa, 553). Unfortunately, he made two mistakes in his list (the angels for Cancer and Libra).

ARIES: MACHIDIEL OR MALAHIDAEL
Dates: March 21–April 20
Color: Red
Gemstone: Ruby, red jasper

People born under the sign of Aries are enthusiastic, competitive, impulsive, independent, pioneering, ambitious, and courageous. They need to keep busy and active, and they are often found in leadership positions. You can call on Machidiel if you need any of these positive Arian qualities.

Machidiel and Malahidael appear frequently in angel lore as different angels, but it seems likely that they are two names for the same angel.

Machidiel is the angel of March and looks after everyone born under the sign of Aries. In the first book of Enoch, he's called Melkejal, the angel who looks after the start of the year. You can call upon Machidiel whenever you need to stand up for what you believe is true. Machidiel will provide you with all the strength and courage you need.

Machidiel is also one of the archangels on the Tree of Life, and is often invoked by men using love magic to attract a suitable female partner. Machidiel is willing to help men and women alike to help them gain the courage they need to express their love to others.

TAURUS: ASMODEL
Dates: April 21–May 21
Color: Green
Gemstone: Emerald, malachite

People born under the sign of Taurus are patient, reliable, practical, conservative, thorough, stable, dependable, and loyal. You can call on Asmodel if you need any of these positive Taurean qualities.

Asmodel governs the month of April and looks after people born under the sign of Taurus. He is considered to be the angel of patience and encourages slow but steady progress. Asmodel loves flowers and nature. This possibly comes from his time as a cherubim guarding the entrance to the Garden of Eden. Unfortunately, after a major uprising in heaven, Asmodel was demoted. Nowadays, he can be called upon for any matters involving friendship, love, and nature. His main interest, though, is helping people remain focused on their goals, especially if by doing this they can steadily improve their financial position.

Gemini: Ambriel
Dates: May 22–June 21
Color: Pale yellow
Gemstone: Agate, banded onyx, striped chalcedony

People born under the sign of Gemini are curious, adaptable, versatile, quick-witted, expressive, and good communicators who are easy to get along with. You can call on Ambriel if you desire any of these positive Geminian qualities.

Ambriel governs the month of May and looks after people born under the sign of Gemini. He is one of the rulers of the choir of thrones. He can be invoked for any matters involving communication. He enjoys helping people who are searching for new work opportunities and responsibilities. Ambriel can also be called upon to repel negativity, no matter where or from whom it comes.

CANCER: MURIEL

Dates: June 22–July 23
Color: Sea green
Gemstone: Green beryl, green turquoise

People born under the sign of Cancer are sensitive, sympathetic, intuitive, tenacious, cautious, protective, nurturing, emotional, and loving. They enjoy peace and tranquility. You can call on Muriel if you desire any of these positive Cancerian qualities.

Muriel governs the month of June and looks after people born under the sign of Cancer. Muriel is the angel of peace and harmony. He especially enjoys helping people who are in close relationships or love nature. Muriel is a useful angel to call upon when you have difficulty controlling your emotions. Muriel is also interested in intuition and the psychic world and is happy to help anyone who is seriously interested in developing their skills.

LEO: VERCHIEL

Dates: July 24–August 23
Color: Yellow
Gemstone: Topaz, zircon

People born under the sign of Leo are self-assured, optimistic, generous, idealistic, proud, dramatic, romantic, courageous, and ambitious. You can call on Verchiel if you wish to develop any of these positive Leonine qualities.

Verchiel governs the month of July and looks after people born under the sign of Leo. Verchiel is also one of the rulers of the choir of powers. According to Papus, the pseudonym of the French occultist Gérard Encausse (1865–1916), Verchiel was also governor of the sun.

Verchiel works well with people seeking friendship and love. He provides energy, enthusiasm, and a huge zest for life. You should also call on Verchiel if you're having major difficulties with family or friends.

VIRGO: HAMALIEL
Dates: August 24–September 22
Color: Apple green
Gemstone: Green chrysoprase

People born under the sign of Virgo are methodical, industrious, reliable, persevering, discriminating, exacting, studious, practical, and analytical. You can call on Hamaliel if you wish to develop any of these positive Virgoan qualities.

Hamaliel governs the month of August and looks after people born under the sign of Virgo. He is ruler of the choir of virtues. Hamaliel can be called upon to help resolve any problems involving logic, attention to detail, and cooperation with others. Hamaliel has a commonsense, practical approach to problems and advocates slow, steady progress rather than trying to accomplish tasks too quickly.

LIBRA: ZURIEL OR URIEL
Dates: September 23–October 23
Color: Green
Gemstone: Green jade, peridot

People born under the sign of Libra are cooperative, diplomatic, companionable, harmonious, sociable, peaceful, refined, charming, and gentle. You can call on Zuriel if you wish to develop any of these positive Libran qualities.

Zuriel governs the month of September and looks after people born under the sign of Libra. Zuriel is also ruler of the choir of principalities. Zuriel can be called upon to create harmonious relationships with others. Zuriel is also the angel of childbirth and is frequently invoked to help ease the pain the mother experiences during labor. *The Book of the Angel Raziel,* dating back to the thirteenth century, advised women to wear an amulet with the name of Zuriel inscribed on it to provide protection during pregnancy and childbirth.

SCORPIO: BARBIEL
Dates: October 24–November 22
Color: Red
Gemstone: Bloodstone, red carnelian

People born under the sign of Scorpio are determined, resourceful, intense, motivated, secretive, possessive, and passionate. You can call on Barbiel if you wish to develop any of these positive Scorpio qualities.

Barbiel governs the month of October and looks after people born under the sign of Scorpio. He is a prince of both the choir of archangels and the choir of virtues. You can call on Barbiel to heal physical and emotional pain. Barbiel also enjoys helping people become more compassionate and understanding. Barbiel is particularly interested in astrology and willing to help people who are developing their intuition.

SAGITTARIUS: ADNACHIEL
Dates: November 23–December 22
Color: Blue
Gemstone: Sapphire, turquoise

People born under the sign of Sagittarius are enthusiastic, optimistic, generous, expansive, philosophical, broad-minded, independent, freedom-loving, and often athletic. You can call on Adnachiel if you wish to develop any of these positive Sagittarian qualities.

Adnachiel governs the month of November and looks after people born under the sign of Sagittarius. Adnachiel and Phaleg are joint rulers of the choir of angels. Adnachiel enjoys working with people who are positive and have a sense of adventure. Adnachiel helps travellers, people who are involved in sporting activities, and people who enjoy investigating new and different ideas. You can call on Adnachiel whenever you're starting a project that might be risky, or are involved in something that takes you out of your comfort zone.

CAPRICORN: HANAEL
Dates: December 23–January 20
Color: Dark blue, black
Gemstone: Tourmaline, black opal

People born under the sign of Capricorn are practical, hardworking, persevering, disciplined, careful, cautious, conscientious, traditional, ambitious, and economical. You can call on Hanael if you wish to develop any of these positive Capricornian qualities.

Hanael governs the month of December and looks after people born under the sign of Capricorn. Hanael is one of the rulers of the choir of principalities and the choir of virtues. Hanael is an angel of joy and harmony, and helps people establish and maintain harmonious relationships with others. He can be called upon to help in any matters involving home and family. Hanael can also be called upon to help with emotional healing.

AQUARIUS: CAMBIEL OR GABRIEL
Dates: January 21–February 19
Color: Sky blue
Gemstone: Aquamarine, lapis lazuli

People born under the sign of Aquarius are idealistic, inventive, imaginative, tolerant, progressive, unconventional, logical, original, and independent. You can call on Cambiel if you wish to develop any of these positive Aquarian qualities.

Cambiel governs the month of January and looks after people born under the sign of Aquarius. Cambiel is especially interested in science, technology, and anything progressive that aids human progress. He helps inventors, and anyone who is doing something new, different, and possibly even eccentric. Cambiel is also compassionate and provides love and comfort to people who are suffering any sort of loss.

PISCES: BARCHIEL
Dates: February 20–March 20
Color: Purple
Gemstone: Amethyst, purple fluorspar

People born under the sign of Pisces are compassionate, sympathetic, kind, impressionable, emotional, empathetic, intuitive, understanding, and tolerant. You can call on Barchiel if you wish to develop any of these positive Piscean qualities.

Barchiel governs the month of February and looks after people born under the sign of Pisces. Barchiel is often called upon by people wanting more good luck in their lives. He asks God to provide blessings to people who need them, and helps them maintain a positive outlook. Gamblers, and people who enjoy games of chance, like Barchiel as he provides abundance and good fortune. His positive outlook extends to home and family life, and he enjoys helping when families find themselves in difficult situations. He encourages people to develop their sense of humor, and to use it to help them handle the inevitable ups and downs of life.

After the discovery of Uranus, Neptune, and Pluto, the archangels Uriel, Asariel, and Azrael were added to the list of planetary angels, thereby creating a completely new arrangement. This is a human construct, of course; I imagine the angels couldn't care less about it. Despite the new arrangement, many magicians prefer working with the original seven archangels. Here is the revised list of planetary archangels:

Aries—Camael—Mars

Taurus—Anael—Venus

Gemini—Raphael—Mercury

Cancer—Gabriel—Moon

Leo—Michael—Sun

Virgo—Raphael—Mercury

Libra—Anael—Venus

Scorpio—Azrael—Pluto

Sagittarius—Zadkiel—Jupiter

Capricorn—Cassiel—Saturn

Aquarius—Uriel—Uranus

Pisces—Asariel—Neptune

In this arrangement, both Anael (Taurus and Libra) and Raphael (Gemini and Virgo) appear twice.

ARCHANGELS OF THE ZODIAC
AND THE MOON

You can access the energies of any of the archangels of the zodiac whenever you wish, as the moon spends approximately two and a half days in each sign every month. This means that if you want to call on Archangel Hanael because you need practicality, discipline, and hard work to complete a particular task, you can find out which days in the current month Hanael will be particularly strong. There are many sites on the Internet that list the different phases of the moon. The one I use is: https://mooncalendar.astro-seek.com/. My astrological diary and daily newspaper also list the movements of the moon.

Keep in mind that the energies of the moon vary depending on whether the moon is waxing (growing larger), waning (decreasing in size), or full. As this can be positive or negative, you'll need to add one of the angels who look after the mansions of the moon. It takes the moon twenty-eight days to complete its lunar cycle, and each day is represented by a different mansion.

Gabriel rules the fifth mansion, which represents the fifth day after the new moon. Gabriel will help your zodiac angel during the first thirteen days of the moon cycle and increase the amount of positive energy available to you.

Ophaniel is in charge of the phases of the moon, and will provide positivity energy from the fourteenth day of the lunar month to the seventeenth.

Amutiel rules the nineteenth mansion and looks after all the days from the eighteenth to the end of the lunar month. This is a time when the moon is waning, and Amutiel helps you let go of anything you no longer need and provides protection from all forms of negativity, including tension and stress.

ARCHANGELS OF THE ZODIAC
CRYSTAL RITUAL

This is a useful way to use a crystal to keep in close contact with the archangel who looks after your sign of the zodiac. The usual way to do this is to find a gemstone or crystal that relates to the color of your sign. However, as there are many lists of color correspondences for the signs of the zodiac, you might prefer to use a clear quartz crystal or a crystal or gemstone that you like instead.

As for color correspondences, there's been a considerable amount of repetition in what has been suggested over the years:

Aries: Pink, red, white, yellow

Taurus: Green, indigo, red-orange

Gemini: Light blue, green, orange, pink, red, light yellow

Cancer: Light blue, gray, green, orange, pink, silver, white, yellow

Leo: Gold, green, orange, red, yellow

Virgo: Black, blue, brown, gold, gray, green, pink, purple, violet, white, yellow

Libra: Black, blue, brown, green, indigo, pink, violet, yellow

Scorpio: Black, blue, brown, gray, green, orange, deep red, yellow

Sagittarius: Black, blue, gold, orange, purple, red, yellow

Capricorn: Black, dark blue, brown, gray, dark green, indigo, red, violet, white

Aquarius: Blue, green, indigo, silver, turquoise, violet, yellow

Pisces: Light blue, green, indigo, lavender, red, violet, white, yellow

Rather than choosing a color first and a gemstone second, you might prefer to go directly to a gemstone that relates to your sign. Here are some suggestions:

Aries: Fire agate, aquamarine, aventurine, bloodstone, carnelian, citrine, diamond, emerald, garnet, hematite, jade, lapis lazuli, fire opal, clear quartz, ruby, sardonyx

Taurus: Carnelian, chrysocolla, chrysoprase, diamond, emerald, iolite, jade, red jasper, kunzite, lapis lazuli, malachite, moss agate, opal, rhodonite, rose quartz, ruby, sapphire, selenite, topaz, blue tourmaline, turquoise

Gemini: Alexandrite, aquamarine, chrysocolla, citrine, emerald, fluorite, howlite, green jasper, lodestone, moonstone, moss agate, clear quartz, sapphire, tiger's eye, topaz

Cancer: Agate, beryl, calcite, carnelian, emerald, moonstone, opal, clear quartz, rose quartz, ruby, sapphire, selenite, red zircon

Leo: Golden beryl, carnelian, citrine, diamond, garnet, jasper, kunzite, labradorite, onyx, peridot, ruby, sapphire, sardonyx, sunstone, tiger's eye, topaz, zircon

Virgo: Agate, amazonite, amethyst, aquamarine, aventurine, carnelian, chrysocolla, diamond, emerald, garnet, jade, pink jasper, lapis lazuli, moss agate, opal, peridot, sapphire, sardonyx, turquoise, red zircon

Libra: Agate, aquamarine, beryl, bloodstone, chrysoprase, citrine, diamond, emerald, iolite, jade, jasper, kunzite, lapis lazuli, malachite, moonstone, rose quartz, sapphire, sunstone, tourmaline

Scorpio: Alexandrite, aquamarine, beryl, bloodstone, carnelian, citrine, red garnet, kunzite, labradorite, malachite, moonstone, obsidian, peridot, rutilated quartz, tourmaline, turquoise, zircon

Sagittarius: Amethyst, azurite, emerald, iolite, labradorite, lapis lazuli, obsidian, opal, ruby, sodalite, sugilite, topaz, turquoise, red zircon

Capricorn: Agate, amethyst, azurite, beryl, bloodstone, carnelian, cat's eye, fluorite, hematite, jet, lapis lazuli, malachite, obsidian, clear quartz, rose quartz, ruby, tiger's eye, turquoise, yellow zircon

Aquarius: Red agate, amethyst, angelite, aquamarine, aventurine, fluorite, hematite, jade, moss agate, onyx, clear quartz, sapphire, turquoise, red zircon

Pisces: Alexandrite, amethyst, aquamarine, bloodstone, blue lace agate, cat's eye, diamond, fluorite, jade, jasper, moonstone, sapphire, sugilite, black tourmaline, turquoise

Once you have your crystal or gemstone, you'll need to consecrate it to enable it to help you make instant contact with your astrological archangel. You can do this by performing a short ritual.

Required:

- A table to act as an altar
- The crystal to be consecrated

- One or two candles (white, or of a color that relates to your zodiac sign)
- A container of water
- A container of salt

Start by placing the table in the center of the area that will contain your magic circle. Place the crystal, salt, and water on it. Ideally, have a bath or shower before you start and change into clean, loose-fitting clothes. I like to wear white colored clothing when performing this ritual.

1. Create the circle you'll be working within. You might like to mark it out with physical objects such as candles or crystals, or you can imagine it in your mind.

2. Step inside the circle and light the candle (or candles) on your altar.

3. Invoke Raphael, Michael, Gabriel, and Uriel to create the circle of protection.

4. Pick up the crystal you're consecrating. Hold it at chest height in the palm of your right hand, resting on the palm of your left hand. Face east and talk to Raphael. Tell him that you wish to consecrate the crystal so you can use it to contact the archangel who relates to your sign of the zodiac. Speak from the heart. The actual words you use are not as important as your intent for the crystal. You might say: "Archangel Raphael, thank you for being here with me. I am grateful for your help, protection, and attention. Today, I ask you to bless this crystal so that I may use it to contact (name of archangel), my astrological angel. Thank you. Thank you. Thank you." Wait until you sense a response. Say one

additional "thank you" and turn to face the south so that you can talk to Archangel Michael.

5. Repeat step 4 with Michael, Gabriel, and Uriel. Once you've received their blessing to your request, hold the crystal against your chest for a few moments, and then place it on your altar. Talk to the crystal. You might say something along the lines of: "I have the blessing of Raphael, Michael, Gabriel, and Uriel, the four greatest archangels, to consecrate you so you may serve as my contact to (name of your astrological archangel)." Pick up the crystal in your right hand. "I now consecrate you with the element of fire." Pass the crystal through the flame of your candle. "I now consecrate you with the element of air." Pass the crystal through the smoke coming from the candle. Place the crystal on your altar. "I now consecrate you with the element of water." Dip your fingers into the container of water and sprinkle some water onto the crystal. "I now consecrate you with the element of earth." Pick up some grains of salt and sprinkle them onto the crystal.

6. Pick up the crystal and place it on the palm of your right hand. Rest your right palm on your left palm, and speak to your crystal. "Thank you for agreeing to help me. You now pledge to call on (your astrological archangel) whenever I request it. I promise to look after you to the best of my ability." Show the crystal to each of the archangels in turn, starting with Raphael, followed by Michael, Gabriel, and Uriel. Finish by standing facing Raphael in the east. Remove your left hand and place it palm downward over the crystal in your right palm.

Rub the crystal gently and talk to your astrological archangel. Notice the instant connection you have with this angel when you're holding the crystal. Thank your astrological archangel for being there for you, and for their willingness to help you.

7. Place the crystal back on your altar. Snuff out the candle, and, when you feel ready, close the circle.

Your crystal is now empowered and ready for use. Carry it with you whenever you can. Any time you feel the need to contact your astrological angel, hold or fondle the crystal for a moment, and you'll instantly be able to communicate with your astrological archangel.

Most crystals can be safely consecrated using the four elements. However, some crystals are adversely affected by water. These are: amber, angelite, azurite, calcite, carnelian, dioptase, galena, halite, hematite, labradorite, malachite, lodestone, lepidolite, mica, moldavite, moonstone, obsidian, opal, pearl, pyrite, selenite, tiger's eye, and turquoise. If you use any of these, pass them over the container of water instead of sprinkling water on them.

ARCHANGELS OF THE MONTH

There are also archangels for each month of the year:

January–Gabriel or Cambiel
Characteristic: Constancy
Birthstone: Garnet

February–Barchiel
Characteristic: Sincerity
Birthstone: Amethyst

March–Machidiel or Malahidael
Characteristic: Courage
Birthstone: Bloodstone

April–Asmodel
Characteristic: Innocence
Birthstone: Diamond

May–Ambriel
Characteristic: Love
Birthstone: Emerald

June–Muriel
Characteristic: Health
Birthstone: Pearl, moonstone, alexandrite

July–Verchiel
Characteristic: Contentment
Birthstone: Ruby

August–Hamaliel
Characteristic: Happy marriage
Birthstone: Sardonyx, peridot

September–Uriel or Zuriel
Characteristic: Clear thinking
Birthstone: Sapphire

October–Barbiel
Characteristic: Hope
Birthstone: Opal, tourmaline

November–Adnachiel or Advachiel
Characteristic: Faithfulness
Birthstone: Topaz, citrine

December–Anael
Characteristic: Wealth
Birthstone: Turquoise, zircon

It can be confusing to have both astrological and monthly archangels. In practice, the archangel doesn't change about a third of the time, and you don't need to be concerned about which archangel to call on. I call on the archangel that looks after my sign for matters relating to my personal future. When making requests for other people, I use the angel of the month if the concern can be resolved within the specific month, or the archangel who looks after their zodiac sign if it might take longer. For requests that do not relate to a single individual, I use the monthly angel or whichever angel I feel would be most intimately involved in the matter.

There's a crystal ritual in chapter nine that will enable you to make instant contact with your astrological angel.

ARCHANGELS OF THE WEEK

People have always been fascinated with the movements of the planets, and because the seven traditional planets (Mars, Mercury, Jupiter, Venus, and Saturn, plus the sun and the moon) were very visible, the ancient Romans associated them with the seven days of the week.

Members of the Merkabah school of Judaic mysticism (it flourished from circa 100 BCE to 1000 CE) believed that archangels looked after these planets. This is not surprising, as people thought that each planet was directed by some form of intelligence as it orbited through the heavens. Over time, a wide variety of other associations such as colors, metals, crystals, chakras, and animals were added to the seven days of the week.

In his book *Collectio Operum*, English Hermetic philosopher, astrologer, and physician Robert Fludd (1574–1637) created a list of seven planetary archangels:

Saturn
Zephkiel: The contemplation of God

Jupiter
Zadkiel: The righteousness of God

Mars
Samael: The severity of God

Sun
Michael: Like unto God

Venus
Hanael: The grace of God

Moon
Gabriel: The strength of God

Mercury
Raphael: The medicine of God

Over the years, a number of different associations have been made, but the archangels of the week and their planetary associations are generally considered to be:

Sunday: Sun–Michael (also Raphael)

Monday: Moon–Gabriel

Tuesday: Mars–Samael (also Uriel and Chamuel)

Wednesday: Mercury—Raphael (also Michael)

Thursday: Jupiter–Zadkiel (also Sachiel and Zachariel)

Friday: Venus–Hanael (also Raguel and Jehudiel)

Saturday: Saturn–Cassiel (also Orifiel and Zaphkiel)

The *Liber Juratus*, sometimes called *The Sworn Book of Honorius*, is a famous thirteenth-century grimoire that magicians referenced across hundreds of years. It gives a clue as to the number of angels who have been associated with the planets and the days of the week. It lists 47 angels for Sunday, 56 for Monday, 52 for Tuesday, 45 for Wednesday, 37 for Thursday, 47 for Friday, and 50 for Saturday.

An ancient tradition says that the soul consists of seven properties that are directed and animated by the seven visible planets (Brewer, 1068). This is related to the Stoic concept of seven senses that were referred to by Philo of Alexandria (ca. 20 BCE–ca. 50 CE) and the Greek physician Claudius Galen (ca. 130 CE–ca. 201 CE) (Possekel, 191).

The first documented evidence of the associations between planets, days of the week, and angels comes from twelfth-century Spain. At that time, European scholars started translating esoteric books from the past and rediscovered many ideas and insights that had been lost. The angels for each day were chosen because the qualities they possessed related to the astrological meanings of the different planets.

Later, in 1801, Francis Barrett described in his book *The Magus* the planetary angels as "those seven spirits which always stand before the face of God" (Barrett, book 2, 56).

Sunday

In Christianity, Judaism, and Islam, Archangel Michael is considered to be the most important angel of all, which makes him the perfect choice for Sunday. In astrology, the sun is the ruler of the sign of Leo. Leo, the lion, is considered the king of the zodiac. Michael is the chief (king) of the choirs of archangels and virtues. He is also the guardian angel and protector of Israel. He is often depicted holding a set of scales, as he's believed to be the angel who'll weigh the souls on Judgment Day.

You can use Michael's energies on a Sunday for motivation, starting new projects, attaining success, enhancing prosperity, and working on health and fitness. It's also a good day for happy communications with fathers and older men.

Monday

Gabriel is the archangel of the moon. Astrologically, the moon has always been associated with creativity, intuition, and childbirth. A creative idea is the birth of something new, so the birth is not restricted solely to childbirth. It was Gabriel who told the Virgin Mary that she'd be giving birth to the son of Christ. Gabriel also dictated the Koran to Muhammad, and this led to the birth of the religion of Islam.

You can use Gabriel's energies on a Monday for home and family concerns, including children and pets, fertility, healing, psychic development, and protection. It's also an excellent day for pleasant communications with mothers and older women.

Tuesday

Samael is the archangel of Mars. Mars has always been considered a war-like planet, and is associated with aggression and strong emotions. The ancient Hebrews considered Samael to be the angel of death. In the Kabbalah, Samael is called "the severity of God." Consequently, people believed that Samael was the angel who was forced to act aggressively and violently when the situation demanded it. Nowadays, Samael is considered an angel of gentleness and protection, but as recently as 150 years ago, Henry Wadsworth Longfellow (1807–1882) described Samael as the angel of death in his poem "The Golden Legend."

You can use Samael's energies on a Tuesday for gaining independence, courage, initiative, passion, and love. It's also a good day for all dealings with younger men, as well as men in the armed forces, police, or fire departments.

Wednesday

Raphael is the archangel of Mercury. Mercury is associated with communication and travel. Raphael accompanied Tobias on a long road trip in the book of Tobit. Raphael is associated with the air signs in astrology. These are Gemini, Libra, and Aquarius. One of the characteristics of the air signs is communication, making Wednesday the perfect day for Raphael.

You can use Raphael's energies on a Wednesday for persuasion, initiative, versatility, and business opportunities. It's also a good day for healing, short-distance travel, working on computers, and learning new technological skills.

Thursday

Sachiel is the archangel of Jupiter. Jupiter relates to generosity, optimism, forward progress, and abundance. Archangel Sachiel is a good fit with Jupiter, as he relates to generosity, prosperity, wealth, and success.

You can use Sachiel's energies on a Thursday for career advancement, expansion, abundance, leadership, loyalty, and all permanent relationships. It's also a good day for all dealings with middle-aged people, and for working on eliminating bad habits and addictions.

Friday

Anael is the archangel of Venus. Venus was the goddess of love, and Anael is associated with affection, love, romance, and sexuality. It's also worth noting that Friday often means a night out for couples who are in love.

You can use Anael's energies on a Friday for enhancing beauty, friendships, love, marriage, and all types of relationships. It's also a good day for steady improvement in any matters of importance, and for all women's health concerns.

Saturday

Cassiel is the archangel of Saturn. The planet Saturn gave us the word "saturnine," which relates well to Archangel Cassiel's slow, ponderous way of working and his sometimes-gloomy temperament. The qualities of the planet Saturn are reliability, responsibility, self-control, discipline, and hard work. These associations also apply to Archangel Cassiel.

You can use Cassiel's energies on a Saturday for gentleness, compassion, self-control, and for overcoming limitations and other restrictions. It's also a good day for dealings with older people and overcoming longstanding problems.

THE PLANETARY HOURS

You might be surprised to learn that there are archangels assigned to every hour of the day. You should use these archangels only when you have something important to do at a specific time. For instance, if you have a dental appointment at two o'clock in the afternoon on a certain day, you might call on the archangel who looks after that particular time for help and protection. You should definitely call on this angel if you're doing something important, such as signing important papers or starting a potentially risky or dangerous task.

The planets are listed 1 to 12 for daytime hours, and 1 to 12 for nighttime hours. Unfortunately, planetary hours don't follow our regular hours. The daytime hours run from sunrise to sunset, and the nighttime hours are the opposite, running from sunset to sunrise. Consequently, the daytime hours are much shorter in winter than they are in summer. My daily newspaper lists sunrise and sunset times every day. You can also obtain this information from a number of websites (I use www.sunrisesunset.com). You need to divide this period of time by twelve to determine how long each planetary hour is for the time of year you happen to be in.

Sunday–daytime hours

1. Michael
2. Anael
3. Raphael
4. Gabriel
5. Cassiel
6. Sachiel
7. Samael
8. Michael
9. Anael
10. Raphael
11. Gabriel
12. Cassiel

Sunday–nighttime hours

1. Sachiel
2. Samael
3. Michael
4. Anael
5. Raphael
6. Gabriel
7. Cassiel
8. Sachiel
9. Samael
10. Michael
11. Anael
12. Raphael

Monday–daytime hours

1. Gabriel
2. Cassiel
3. Sachiel
4. Samael
5. Michael
6. Anael
7. Raphael
8. Gabriel
9. Cassiel
10. Sachiel
11. Samael
12. Michael

Monday–nighttime hours

1. Anael
2. Raphael
3. Gabriel
4. Cassiel
5. Sachiel
6. Samael
7. Michael
8. Anael
9. Raphael
10. Gabriel
11. Cassiel
12. Sachiel

Tuesday–daytime hours

1. Samael
2. Michael
3. Anael
4. Raphael
5. Gabriel
6. Cassiel
7. Sachiel
8. Samael
9. Michael
10. Anael
11. Raphael
12. Gabriel

Tuesday–nighttime hours

1. Cassiel
2. Sachiel
3. Samael
4. Michael
5. Anael
6. Raphael
7. Gabriel
8. Cassiel
9. Sachiel
10. Samael
11. Michael
12. Anael

Wednesday–daytime hours

1. Raphael
2. Gabriel
3. Cassiel
4. Sachiel
5. Samael
6. Michael
7. Anael
8. Raphael
9. Gabriel
10. Cassiel
11. Sachiel
12. Samael

Wednesday–nighttime hours

1. Michael
2. Anael
3. Raphael
4. Gabriel
5. Cassiel
6. Sachiel
7. Samael
8. Michael
9. Anael
10. Raphael
11. Gabriel
12. Cassiel

Thursday–daytime hours

1. Sachiel
2. Samael
3. Michael
4. Anael
5. Raphael
6. Gabriel
7. Cassiel
8. Sachiel
9. Samael
10. Michael
11. Anael
12. Raphael

Thursday–nighttime hours

1. Gabriel
2. Cassiel
3. Sachiel
4. Samael
5. Michael
6. Anael
7. Raphael
8. Gabriel
9. Cassiel
10. Sachiel
11. Samael
12. Michael

Friday–daytime hours

1. Anael
2. Raphael
3. Gabriel
4. Cassiel
5. Sachiel
6. Samael
7. Michael
8. Anael
9. Raphael
10. Gabriel
11. Cassiel
12. Sachiel

Friday–nighttime hours

1. Samael
2. Michael
3. Anael
4. Raphael
5. Gabriel
6. Cassiel
7. Sachiel
8. Samael
9. Michael
10. Anael
11. Raphael
12. Gabriel

Saturday–daytime hours

1. Cassiel
2. Sachiel
3. Samael
4. Michael
5. Anael
6. Raphael
7. Gabriel
8. Cassiel
9. Sachiel
10. Samael
11. Michael
12. Anael

Saturday–nighttime hours

1. Raphael
2. Gabriel
3. Cassiel
4. Sachiel
5. Samael
6. Michael
7. Anael
8. Raphael
9. Gabriel
10. Cassiel
11. Sachiel
12. Samael

As you can see, you are constantly surrounded by archangels of the zodiac, months, days, and hours. This means you have access to the particular angelic energies at almost any time of the day or night. It can be helpful to create a list of the angels who are available to help you at any time that is likely to be important. This will enable you to enhance your life by arranging meetings and appointments at times that are most beneficial for you.

HOW TO CONTACT YOUR ASTROLOGICAL ANGELS

Obviously, you must have a purpose in contacting your astrological archangels. There's no point in conducting a ritual simply to say hello. You could conduct a ritual to thank them for looking after you, but it is more useful to have a specific aim in mind before calling on them.

You'll need four candles: one each of yellow, green, blue and red. These will be used to mark out the magic circle and to indicate the cardinal directions. You will also need an offering to give to the angel(s) you call on. A slice of freshly baked cake and a glass of wine or fruit juice are ideal. Place all of these on a table (altar) in the center of your circle before starting.

Before commencing the ritual, decide on the specific angel you wish to talk with, and the best time of day to conduct the ritual. You can conduct a ritual at any time, but it is best to perform them when the moon is waxing (growing) rather than waning. The best times of day for you are the hours that relate to your astrological angel.

It is not always easy to decide on the correct angel. If you are a Libran, for instance, you might choose Anael and perform the ritual at the fifth daytime hour on a Saturday, as that also relates to Anael. However, in this example, you might consider calling on Barbiel, if your birthday is in the first few weeks of October. If you decide on Barbiel, you can still use the planetary hours associated with Anael. If your concern can be resolved within the month, you might choose the angel of the month. Choose your astrological angel for matters that cannot be resolved as quickly.

Here's another example. Let's assume your birthday is on March 3, which makes you a Piscean. You could choose Asariel, the angel that looks after your sign. Alternatively, you might choose Machidiel or Malahidael, as they look after the month of March. You might choose to perform the ritual on Thursday, ruled by Sachiel, as he looks after Pisceans. If it isn't possible to perform the ritual on a Thursday, you could perform it at any of the hours dedicated to Sachiel. If your concern is serious but you feel confident it will be resolved in the next few weeks, you might decide on

Machidiel and perform the ritual at the second nighttime hour on a Tuesday.

Here is the basic format of a typical ritual to contact the astrological angels:

Required:

- A table
- Four candles (ideally one each: yellow, red, blue, green. Use white candles if you don't have colored ones.)
- A slice of cake or a tasty substitute, to eat during the ritual
- A glass of wine or fruit juice

1. If possible, have a bath or shower before starting the ritual. Change into clean, comfortable, loose-fitting clothes.

2. Create a circle of protection around your altar. Place the yellow candle in the east, the red one in the south, the blue one in the west, and the green one in the north.

3. Walk around the circle again, lighting the candles. Start with the yellow candle in the east and move around the circle in a clockwise direction lighting the candles in order.

4. Stand in the center of your circle. Pick up the slice of cake and hold it at chest height in your cupped hands. Face east and say out loud: "I offer you (name of the angel you want to communicate with) this cake as a token of my love and respect." Repeat this at the other cardinal points, offering the cake each time to the same angel. Face east again, and slowly eat the cake. As you do this, visualize that your request has already been granted, and that the desired future is already present.

5. After eating the cake, repeat step five using the glass of wine (or fruit juice). Place the wine glass on the ground, or on your altar, when you have finished drinking it.

6. You are now ready to summon the specific angel you want to talk with. Face east, close your eyes, and say the angel's name seven times out loud. Picture the angel you are invoking in your mind. It makes no difference what image comes to you—some people picture an angel with large wings; others sense colors, smells, sounds, and even shapes. Others don't sense anything in particular but have a sense that the angel is there with them.

7. Once you're aware that your angel is with you, thank him for coming to your aid, tell him your request in as much detail as possible, and then wait silently for a response. You may hear spoken words, thoughts might appear in your mind, or you might feel that everything will work out the way it should. No matter what response you receive, thank the angel sincerely.

8. At this point, you can ask further questions, or discuss other matters with the angel. You're likely to sense when the angel is ready to return to the celestial realms. Thank him/her and say goodbye. Call out a final "thank you" and close the circle by putting out the candles in the usual east, south, west, north order.

9. Rest for a few minutes before carrying on with your day. Even though you consumed food and drink during the ritual, eat a few nuts and raisins, and drink some water afterward to ground yourself and restore your energy.

CHAPTER TEN

ARCHANGELS OF THE SEVEN RAYS

The seven rays are universal energies expressed by the universal life force, and they have a profound influence on peoples' souls. Each ray has its own particular energy that produces one of the seven different types of souls. The concept of the seven rays dates back at least two thousand years (Walker, 253). Early Christian artists frequently portrayed the dove of the Holy Ghost with seven rays of color emanating from it.

Members of the Theosophical Society believe that everything in the entire solar system belongs to one of the seven rays. Alice A. Bailey (1880–1949), the American occultist, wrote: "Each vibrating unit of energy can say: I am part of a divine whole, which in its septenary [sevenfold] nature expresses to love and life of the One Reality, colored by one of the seven qualities of love of Deity and responsive to other qualities" (Bailey, 42).

Here are the qualities of each ray. As you read them, see if you can determine which ray or rays you are working on. In this lifetime, you might be focused primarily on one specific ray, or you may be working on two, three, or even all of them simultaneously.

First Ray:
Ray of Power and Will
Archangel: Michael
Color: Blue, red
Gem: Diamond

The first ray is sometimes called the Ray of Deity, as its purpose is to confirm the existence of the Divine on a physical level. This ray provides courage, self-reliance, ambition, and willpower. It also gives leadership qualities, a sense of purpose, and the ability to come up with good ideas and to make them happen. This ray can provide ultimate wisdom. Archangel Michael, as angel of the first ray, will be happy to help you develop these qualities if you ask for them.

Second Ray:
Ray of Love and Wisdom
Archangel: Jophiel
Color: Yellow, blue
Gem: Sapphire

People working on this ray are able to see themselves from the viewpoint of the Divine, and this enables kindness, compassion, love, and wisdom to develop. The second ray provides insight, generosity, sympathy, and diplomacy. It also helps people to develop empathy, intuition, tact, gentleness, and a positive outlook on life. Archangel Jophiel, the angel of the second ray, will be happy to help you develop these qualities if you ask.

THIRD RAY:
RAY OF ACTIVE INTELLIGENCE
Archangel: Chamuel
Color: Yellow, pink
Gem: Emerald

This ray enables the Divine to send thoughts and ideas to people working on this ray. The third ray provides creativity, understanding, adaptability, and perception. It also helps people to plan ahead, communicate well, and succeed in life. Once they have achieved their goals, they frequently use their skills to help others. Archangel Chamuel, angel of the third ray, will be happy to help you develop these qualities if you ask.

FOURTH RAY:
RAY OF HARMONY, BEAUTY, AND ART
Archangel: Gabriel
Color: White
Gem: Jasper

The fourth ray provides harmony, stability, and inner peace. However, this essential harmony is most likely to come through conflict. This ray enables the Divine to send people on this ray the heart's desires that they need to manifest. It also enables people to develop their sense of humor, express themselves effectively, and develop their creative abilities. If you ask her, Archangel Gabriel, angel of the fourth ray, will happily help you to develop these skills.

FIFTH RAY:
RAY OF CONCRETE
KNOWLEDGE AND SCIENCE
Archangel: Raphael
Color: Orange, green
Gem: Topaz

People on the fifth ray have access to knowledge from the past, present, and future, and also have the ability to make good use of it. The fifth ray provides patience, logic, and the ability to analyze and discern. It enables people to use their brains effectively, and to be inventive, precise, and exact. Archangel Raphael will be happy to help you develop these qualities if you ask.

SIXTH RAY:
RAY OF DEVOTION AND IDEALISM
Archangel: Uriel
Color: Purple, gold
Gem: Ruby

The sixth ray enters the human body as intuition, and enables the Divine to send pure unconditional love and support to the person. This ray provides enthusiasm, optimism, positivity, loyalty, sincerity, and devotion. It also gives people persistence, drive, and the ability to motivate others. It encourages people to explore and investigate anything that is hidden or unknown. Archangel Raphael will be happy to help you develop these qualities if you ask.

SEVENTH RAY:
RAY OF ORDER AND CEREMONIAL MAGIC
Archangel: Zadkiel
Color: Violet
Gem: Amethyst

The seventh ray provides people with the ability to express themselves effectively, create order out of chaos, and to turn their hopes and dreams into reality. It encourages people to be kind, honorable, and loyal. Archangel Zadkiel will be happy to help you develop these qualities if you ask.

WHAT RAY ARE YOU ON?

You may have discovered which ray you are working on in this lifetime while reading about them. If you aren't sure which ray, or rays, you're on, here's a questionnaire that will help you determine which areas to focus on.

Answer each question with a score of 0 to 5. 5 means you agree strongly with the question, and 0 means the question is not relevant for you in this lifetime.

Here are the questions:

1. Do you like to be in charge?

   0   1   2   3   4   5

2. Are you tactful and diplomatic?

   0   1   2   3   4   5

3. Do you enjoy discussing your ideas with others?

   0   1   2   3   4   5

4. Do you find it easy to mediate with others?

   0   1   2   3   4   5

5. Are you a clear, logical thinker?

   0   1   2   3   4   5

6. Are you loyal?

   0   1   2   3   4   5

7. Can you create and maintain system and order?

   0   1   2   3   4   5

8. Are you a leader?

   0   1   2   3   4   5

9. Are you sympathetic and compassionate?

   0   1   2   3   4   5

10. Are you broad-minded?

    0   1   2   3   4   5

11. Do you have a good imagination?

    0   1   2   3   4   5

12. Did you enjoy mathematics at school?

    0   1   2   3   4   5

13. Are you an optimist?

    0   1   2   3   4   5

14. Do you enjoy complicated, detailed work?

    0   1   2   3   4   5

15. Are you an independent thinker?

    0   1   2   3   4   5

16. Are you tolerant of others?

    0   1   2   3   4   5

17. Are you good at dealing with money?

    0   1   2   3   4   5

18. Do you have an aesthetic sense, and appreciate beauty?

    0   1   2   3   4   5

19. Do you enjoy researching and analyzing?

    0   1   2   3   4   5

20. Are you single-minded?

    0   1   2   3   4   5

21. Do you enjoy ritual and ceremony?

    0   1   2   3   4   5

22. Do you have a strong sense of where you are going in your life?

    0   1   2   3   4   5

23. Do you love humanity as a whole?

    0   1   2   3   4   5

24. Do you enjoy analyzing problems and creating effective solutions?

    0   1   2   3   4   5

25. Are you growing spiritually as you progress through life?

    0   1   2   3   4   5

26. Are you a logical thinker, who can put all emotions to one side while working on a problem?

    0   1   2   3   4   5

27. Are you an idealist?

    0   1   2   3   4   5

28. Are you able to manifest your desires?

    0   1   2   3   4   5

29. Are you courageous?

    0   1   2   3   4   5

30. Are you able to remain serene and worry-free when problems occur in your life?

    0   1   2   3   4   5

31. Are you constantly full of ideas?

    0   1   2   3   4   5

32. Are you able to captivate others?

    0   1   2   3   4   5

33. Are you as good with your hands as you are with your mind?

    0   1   2   3   4   5

34. Are you able to focus on a task and see it to completion?

    0   1   2   3   4   5

35. Do you see yourself as powerful?

    0   1   2   3   4   5

36. Do you stand up for what you believe in?

    0   1   2   3   4   5

37. Are you good at teaching others the skills that you possess?

    0   1   2   3   4   5

38. Are you, or would you make, a good businessperson?

   0   1   2   3   4   5

39. Can you express yourself well with words on paper?

   0   1   2   3   4   5

40. Do you have any technical skills?

   0   1   2   3   4   5

41. Do you have a strong faith?

   0   1   2   3   4   5

42. Do you enjoy ritual and ceremony?

   0   1   2   3   4   5

Once you've completed the questionnaire, you can find out which ray or rays you are on.

Questions 1, 8, 15, 22, 29, and 36 relate to the first ray.

Questions 2, 9, 16, 23, 30, and 37 relate to the second ray.

Questions 3, 10, 17, 24, 31, and 38 relate to the third ray.

Questions 4, 11, 18, 25, 32, and 39 relate to the fourth ray.

Questions 5, 12, 19, 26, 33, and 40 relate to the fifth ray.

Questions 6, 13, 20, 27, 34, and 41 relate to the sixth ray.

Questions 7, 14, 21, 28, 35, and 42 relate to the seventh ray.

You may find that one ray is much stronger than the others. This means you are primarily on this ray. If two or three rays are stronger than the others, this shows that you are learning the lessons of these rays in this lifetime.

It's possible for all the rays to be approximately equal in strength. This is unusual, but it can happen. If this occurs, reread the descriptions of the seven rays to see if you can determine which is the strongest and consequently your primary ray.

Discovering your ray (or rays) will help you discover your purpose in this lifetime, and which archangel will be the most useful one for you to work with to achieve it.

How to Work with the Archangels of Your Ray

Once you know which archangel, or archangels, you need to work with, you need to set aside some time every now and again to relax and think about your purpose in this lifetime.

Required:

- Anything that relates to your angel, such as a gemstone, an illustration, or something that happens to be the same color as your ray. This could be a candle, an item of clothing, an ornament, or even a swatch of cloth.

1. Sit down comfortably, close your eyes, and relax by taking several slow, deep breaths. Visualize yourself relaxing deeply with each exhalation. If you are using a gemstone, hold it in your left hand during the ritual.

2. Visualize a pure white light descending from above and filling your entire being with divine energy. When your body is filled to overflowing, sense the white light surrounding you and filling the room you're within.

3. When you feel fully relaxed, start talking to the archangel of your ray. You might start by telling the angel about the day you've just had, and then gradually start talking about your hopes and dreams. Mention the purpose indicated by your ray, and say whether or not you

feel aligned to it. If you're on the fifth ray, for instance, you might feel that as you've always been patient, you've already learned the lesson of this ray. In this instance, Archangel Raphael, who is responsible for the fifth ray, might tell you that although you're patient, you still have a great deal of work to do before you become skilled at accessing information from the past, present, and future.

4. Speak for as long as you need to pass on all your fears, doubts, and concerns about the ray you are on. When you stop speaking, remain silent and wait for a response. This could come as words, either spoken or in thoughts that appear in your mind. You might feel a sense of encouragement or a feeling that you are on track. You might have a feeling of deep peace in your heart and mind. You may feel that you received no response at all. However, in time you'll realize that your archangel was working for you. You might receive information in a dream. You might hear a song on the radio with lyrics that answer your concerns. You might feel more optimistic about the future and where you are going in your life.

5. No matter what sort of response you receive, thank your archangel for making time to listen to you. If necessary, express a hope that you'll receive a message in the next few days. Express your gratitude for the love your archangel has for you, and say goodbye.

6. Sit quietly for a few moments, and then count slowly from one to five. Open your eyes and get up when you feel ready. If you're performing this ritual in bed

at night, there's no need to open your eyes and get out of bed. Allow yourself to fall asleep, confident that your archangel is protecting you and will provide you with the answers you seek.

If you're going to carry on with your day once the ritual is over, have something to eat and drink to make sure that you're grounded before doing anything else.

You can perform this ritual as often as you wish. With practice, you'll find you'll be able to relax quickly and start communicating with the archangel of your ray within a minute or two.

ARCHANGELS OF THE CHAKRAS

All living things are surrounded by an energy field called the aura. Inside the aura are a number of energy centers called chakras. *Chakra* is a Sanskrit word that means "wheel" or "vortex," as the chakras are visualized as swirling wheels of positive energy. The chakras distribute divine energy throughout the body. They vitalize and stimulate the physical body, and provide spiritual energy to help human beings grow and develop inwardly.

Ideally, this energy flows smoothly and easily throughout the chakra system. Blockages and disturbances create either excessive or deficient energy. Strong emotions such as anger, lust, jealousy, and fear can cause blockages in the chakra system.

The chakras cannot be seen, and exist in the same way that thoughts and emotions do. If you've ever been so overcome with emotion that you thought your heart would burst, you've experienced your heart chakra. If you've ever been so excited that you couldn't express yourself because your throat was constricted, you've felt your throat chakra.

There are seven main chakras aligned along the spinal column. Each is governed by an archangel. Each chakra is also related to one of the endocrine glands that are essential in maintaining energy, harmony, and stability because they provide the necessary hormones to maintain a healthy body.

ROOT CHAKRA

Location: Base of the spine, coccyx
Element: Earth
Color: Red
Gland: Adrenal
Gemstone: Red coral
Planet: Mars
Archangel: Sandalphon
Essential oils: Benzoin, patchouli, vetiver

The root chakra's functions are survival, grounding, security, contact with the earth, and physical energy. Until people's survival needs have been taken of, they're unable to focus on other aspects of their lives. This chakra is in balance when they feel grounded, supported, and safe. Sandalphon helps people restore this balance and start moving forward again.

SACRAL CHAKRA

Location: Four finger widths below the navel
Element: Water
Color: Orange
Gland: Gonads, prostate
Gemstone: Pearl
Planet: Moon
Archangels: Gabriel, Chamuel
Essential oils: Dill, geranium, hyssop, jasmine, marjoram, neroli, rose,
sandalwood

The functions of the sacral chakra are the emotions, sexuality, pleasure, and creativity. When this chakra is in balance, the person will be outgoing, creative, and feel comfortable with their sexuality. When the sacral chakra is blocked, the person is likely to be greedy, angry, lustful, and overly emotional. Because the sacral chakra is related to the water element, many people with blocked sacral chakras weep frequently. Archangels Gabriel and Chamuel are willing to help resolve this.

SOLAR PLEXUS CHAKRA

Location: Two finger widths above the navel
Element: Fire
Color: Yellow
Gland: Pancreas
Gemstone: Ruby
Planet: Sun
Archangels: Uriel, Michael, Jophiel
Essential oils: Benzoin, bergamot, chamomile, cypress, dill, elemi, fennel, hyssop, juniper, lemon, marjoram, neroli, sage

The functions of the solar plexus chakra are willpower, confidence, emotional power, intelligence, love, physical energy, healing, and transformation. When this chakra is in balance, people feel self-respect, and are compassionate with themselves and others. When people get nervous, they lack power or control, and get butterflies in their stomachs. Calling on archangels Uriel, Michael, or Jophiel will help relieve this.

HEART CHAKRA

Location: Center of the breastbone
Element: Air
Color: Green
Gland: Thymus
Gemstone: Sapphire
Planet: Venus
Archangels: Raphael, Chamuel

Essential oils: Benzoin, bergamot, cinnamon, clove, elemi, gera-nium, immortelle, lavender, lime, mandarin, neroli, palmarose, rose, sandalwood

The functions of the heart chakra are love, family, devotion, compassion, healing, and balance. When this chakra is in balance, people experience joy, love, gratitude, and compassion. Many people have blocked heart chakras caused by emotional trauma. A good example is someone who has experienced a major loss but has failed to go through the necessary grieving process. Archangels Raphael and Chamuel will help the healing process.

THROAT CHAKRA

Location: Throat, at level of the larynx
Element: Ether
Color: Blue
Gland: Thyroid, parathyroid
Gemstone: Diamond
Planet: Jupiter
Archangel: Michael
Essential oils: Benzoin, blue chamomile, cajeput, cypress, elemi, eucalyptus, myrrh, palmarose, rosemary, sage, yarrow

The functions of the throat chakra are speaking, communication, creativity, and channeling. When this chakra is in balance, people express themselves clearly, and are able to articulate their truth. When the throat chakra is blocked, people become shy and uncommunicative. In this situation, Archangel Michael will give the necessary courage to speak the truth. Conversely, when this chakra is wide open, people talk too much and fail to listen. Michael is happy to provide help for this situation, too.

BROW OR THIRD EYE CHAKRA
Location: Center of forehead, between the eyebrows
Element: Light
Color: Indigo
Gland: Pituitary
Gemstone: Topaz
Planet: Venus
Archangels: Gabriel, Jophiel
Essential oils: Basil, carrot seed, clary sage, ginger, melissa, peppermint, pine, rosemary, rosewood

The functions of the brow chakra are clairvoyance, psychic and intuitive perception, and imagination. This chakra is also related to wisdom, higher consciousness, dreams, memory, and vision. When this chakra is in balance, people are willing to listen to other points of view, and enjoy pursuing their goals. When the brow chakra is out of balance, people experience eye strain, sinus problems, and headaches. They're also inclined to be stubborn and temperamental.

CROWN CHAKRA
Location: Top of the head
Element: Thought
Color: Violet
Gland: Pineal
Gemstone: Emerald
Planet: Saturn
Archangel: Zadkiel
Essential oils: Cedarwood, elemi, frankincense, jasmine, neroli, rose, rosewood

The most important function of the crown chakra is to maintain a connection with the Divine. Its other functions are spirituality, intuition, illumination, consciousness, understanding, inner knowledge, acceptance, and awareness. Information enters the crown chakra and is then distributed to the other chakras to enable the person to receive the maximum benefit provided by these positive qualities. When the crown chakra is in balance, people trust their inner guidance, and have a strong connection with the Divine. When this chakra is out of balance, people tend to be rigid, paranoid, and experience a sense of isolation.

CHAKRA BALANCING WITH THE ARCHANGELS

Chakra balancing is a form of energy healing that fills our bodies and minds with vital life energy. If you are aware that a particular chakra is out of balance, hold a crystal that relates to it on your body, over the area of the specific chakra. Ask the archangel that relates to this chakra to balance and restore it. Visualize this happening for three or four minutes. After this, thank the archangel, and remove the crystal. You might like to use candles, incense, and essential oils as well. If you wish, you could play a favorite piece of gentle music, too.

After the ritual, carry the crystal with you, and touch or caress it whenever you feel the need for extra stimulation or energy. Recharge it each time you perform the ritual.

Chakra Balancing Meditation

This is a meditation that uses the archangels to balance all seven chakras. You'll need about thirty minutes of uninterrupted time. Wear loose-fitting clothes, and make sure the room is pleasantly warm.

1. Lie on your back, eyes closed and your hands by your sides. Take several slow deep breaths, and allow your body to relax as much as possible. When you feel suffi-

ciently relaxed, visualize a pure white light descending from above, and surrounding you with love and protection. Enjoy the feeling of being totally surrounded by this pure white light, and then silently ask Archangel Michael to come and protect you while you're performing the meditation. When you sense the presence of Michael, thank him for joining you and tell him that you're balancing your chakras.

2. Focus your attention on your root chakra. Imagine that part of your body surrounded by a beautiful red glow of light. If you feel it will help you visualize better, place your hands over this area as well. Ask Michael to introduce you to Archangel Sandalphon. When Sandalphon appears, ask him to cleanse, restore, and balance your root chakra. As he does this, you'll gradually start to experience a sensation of security as you become well-grounded again.

3. Once Sandalphon has finished, thank him as he moves to one side. Focus on the area of your sacral chakra, and visualize it surrounded by a vivid orange glow. If you wish, place your hands over this area. Ask Michael to introduce you to Archangel Chamuel, the angel of unconditional love. Relax and allow Chamuel to balance, revitalize, and restore your sacral chakra.

4. Allow Chamuel as much time as necessary. You'll feel a sense of happiness and contentment as Chamuel balances this chakra. When he's finished, thank him for his help, and then move your attention up to your solar plexus chakra. Imagine this area surrounded by a beautiful yellow radiance. Place your hands on your solar

plexus chakra if you wish. Ask Michael to introduce you to Archangel Uriel, the great archangel of peace. Ask Uriel to balance this chakra, and feel all of the pent-up hurts and fears being replaced with peace and harmony as he restores your solar plexus chakra.

5. Thank Uriel when he's finished, and focus on your heart chakra. Visualize it surrounded by a beautiful, calming, peaceful green. Place your hands over the chakra if you wish. Ask Michael to introduce you to Raphael, archangel of wholeness and healing. Ask Raphael to balance and heal your heart chakra. Balancing this chakra can be an emotional experience. There's no need to be concerned if this occurs, as releasing these emotions is healing and cathartic. You'll feel a sense of love and the interconnectedness of all living things when this chakra is balanced.

6. Focus on your throat chakra and visualize it surrounded by a clear blue light. If you wish, place your hands on your throat. This is the chakra that Michael looks after. Relax, and let him balance and restore this chakra for you. You'll feel a sense of peace and contentment as he does this. Thank him for his help once you sense he is finished.

7. When you sense that Michael is done working on your throat chakra, allow your attention to focus on your brow chakra. Visualize this area surrounded by a pure, deep indigo color. Place your hands on your brow, if you wish. Ask Michael to introduce you to Gabriel, archangel of the soul. Feel your intuition expanding as Gabriel balances your brow (third eye) chakra.

8. Thank Archangel Gabriel, and once she's moved to one side, focus on your crown chakra. Place your hands on top of your head, if you feel it will help you visualize this chakra. Imagine the top of your head completely surrounded with an intense violet glow. Ask Michael to introduce you to Archangel Zadkiel, archangel of forgiveness. Ask Zadkiel to balance your crown chakra, and feel a sensation of peace and tranquility spread throughout your entire body as Zadkiel balances this chakra. Thank Zadkiel once he has completed this task.

9. Now it's time to thank each archangel individually. Visualize yourself surrounded by a pure red energy as you thank Archangel Sandalphon. Visualize yourself surrounded by a powerful orange light as you thank Chamuel. Continue thanking each of the archangels in turn, while imagining yourself being surrounded by each color of the rainbow in turn.

10. Say goodbye to all the archangels and visualize them disappearing from view. Lie quietly for a few minutes and relive the entire experience in your mind. When you feel ready, count up to five and open your eyes. Lie quietly for another minute and then get up.

You'll feel revitalized in mind, body, and soul after this meditation. Your chakras will be balanced, and you'll be full of all the joys of life. You can perform this meditation as often as you wish, ideally about once a week. You should perform it more frequently if you're experiencing tension, stress, or any kind of emotional difficulty.

Here is a simpler and faster way to balance your chakras. I prefer the method we've just described, but the following method can be done anywhere, at any time, as long as you're able to close your eyes for a few minutes. Consequently, you could even perform it while seated in public transportation or waiting for a movie to start.

1. Sit down comfortably and close your eyes. Take a few slow deep breaths, and allow your body to relax.

2. Visualize Archangel Michael (or any other archangel you wish) standing several feet in front of you. He's holding a powerful spotlight. As you think of your root chakra, Michael directs a strong ray of red at the area of your root chakra. You can sense the chakra responding to this powerful dose of red energy.

3. When you feel your root chakra has received enough attention, think of your sacral chakra. Immediately Michael directs the ray of the light to this area, and you notice the color of the light has changed to orange. Again, sense this orange energy revitalizing and restoring your sacral chakra until you feel it has been restored to perfect balance.

4. Continue moving up the chakras, noticing that the ray from Archangel Michael's spot light changes color the second you start thinking of the next chakra.

5. When Archangel Michael has finished working on your crown chakra, mentally scan all seven chakras before thanking him for his help and support. Say goodbye to him and visualize him fading from sight.

6. Silently count from one to five and open your eyes.

ESSENTIAL OILS AND THE ARCHANGELS

Many people become aware of an indescribably beautiful scent shortly before an angelic appearance. This scent can linger for thirty or forty minutes after the angel has gone. As angels enjoy pleasant fragrances, it's a good idea to use oils, scents, and perfumes to attract them to us. Essential oils are convenient and provide a useful way of doing this. They're readily available from herb stores, new age stores, some pharmacies, and online. Essential oils are used for many purposes, including aromatherapy, and because they're healing and encourage spiritual growth, they're also useful in encouraging angelic communication.

There are specific oils that work well with the different chakras and can be used with the archangels who look after the specific chakras. Feel free to experiment with different oils, as it's important that you enjoy the scents you use.

Angelica seed is a particularly useful oil for attracting the angelic realms, and it may have even gained its name because of this. This oil helps people open up their intuition and strengthen their faith.

How to Use Essential Oils

Essential oils are highly concentrated plant extracts, and can cause harm if not used carefully. They are not recommended for young children, pregnant or breastfeeding women, and elderly people. If you're taking any medications, check with your doctor before using them. Essential oils should be diluted with a carrier oil if you intend to apply them directly to your skin. This is especially important if you have sensitive skin. Err on the side of caution if you have any doubts or concerns. The safest way of using them for our purposes is to use an electric oil burner.

Electric oil burners can be obtained anywhere where aroma-therapy supplies are sold. They're convenient, safe, and create just enough heat to enable the essential oil to release its scent. All you need do is add eight to ten drops of the oil to the burner before turning it on. These burners are the easiest and safest way to use essential oils.

You can also obtain traditional oil burners that are heated by a candle. Obviously, these need to be treated with great care and should never be left unsupervised.

You can give yourself a quick boost with the scent by adding up to ten drops of oil to a bowl of steaming water. Cover your head and the bowl with a towel, and breathe in the scent in the vapor for two or three minutes.

You can also add a drop or two of an essential oil to a handkerchief or pillow. Most essential oils will not create a stain, but you should be careful when using darker-colored oils such as vetiver and patchouli.

In the next chapter we'll look at how to experience angel visitations in your dreams and how to work with and make good use of lucid dreams.

DREAMING WITH THE ARCHANGELS

Throughout history, people have been fascinated with their dreams. The Chester Beatty papyri contains records of dream interpretations dating back almost four thousand years. The first known book on dream interpretation was *Oneirocritica,* written in the second century CE by Artemidorus. Many sacred texts, including the Bible, contain accounts of people's visions and dreams with angels. These include Jacob's dream of a ladder between heaven and earth, with angels climbing up and down it (Genesis 28:12–15). Joseph received three important messages from angels in his dreams. The first one occurred when the angel of the Lord told him "That which is conceived in her is of the Holy Ghost" (Matthew 1:20). The angel of the Lord appeared again and told Joseph to "take the young child and his mother, and flee into Egypt, and be thou there until I bring thee word: for Herod will seek the young child to destroy him" (Matthew 2:13). After King Herod died, Joseph had another dream in which the angel of the Lord said: "Arise, and take the young child and his mother, and go into the land of Israel: for they are dead which sought the young child's life" (Matthew 2:20).

At the age of sixteen, Saint Patrick (ca. 385–ca. 461) was captured by pirates and sold to an Antrim chief in Ireland. After six years of slavery, he received a dream message from God and escaped. Some years later, he had another dream in which an angel appeared to him and told him to return to Ireland as a missionary. It took him many years of study before he was able to return and introduce Christianity to the Irish people.

When Muhammad (ca. 570–632), the founder of Islam, was forty years old, he saw Gabriel in his dreams. Gabriel dictated the Koran to him in a series of visions, marking the start of the religion of Islam.

The Church of Jesus Christ of Latter-Day Saints also began after the angel Moroni appeared to Joseph Smith (1805–1844) in a dream and told him where the engraved golden tablets containing the Book of Mormon were buried.

Everybody dreams, and we usually have four or five dream periods every night. However, these dreams quickly fade from our memories. Researchers at the University of Chicago conducted an experiment with ten volunteers that demonstrated just how quickly our dreams are forgotten. The experiment lasted for fifty-one nights, and the volunteers were woken up at different times. When they were woken up during periods of REM (rapid eye movement) sleep, they were able to provide detailed descriptions of their dreams on forty-six out of fifty-four occasions. However, when they were woken five minutes after the REM stage, they were unable to provide detailed accounts, though fragments of dreams were recalled on nine of eleven occasions. When they were woken ten or more minutes after the REM stage, only one dream fragment was obtained from twenty-six occasions (Oswald, 68).

Most people are woken up by alarm clocks and have to immediately get out of bed and get ready for the day. Consequently, even if they wake up with memories of a dream that they've had, it disappears in seconds once they start their day. It's much easier to remember your dreams when you wake up naturally and have time to think about them before getting out of bed.

It can be useful to keep a dream diary by your bed so that you can record your dreams before they're lost forever. Although many people nowadays record their dreams into their phones, I've always written my dreams down in exercise books. Over the years they've created a valuable record of what was going on in my subconscious mind. When I read over these dreams, I can see how they've helped and guided me in different areas of my life. Sometimes dreams that didn't appear to make any sense when I recorded them became obvious when I read them again weeks or months later. A dream diary can also confirm the accuracy of your precognitive dreams. Up to ten percent of your dreams relate to future events.

Because everyone dreams every night, most people take their dreams for granted, and don't try to recapture their dream memories when they wake up. Fortunately, it's not hard to become better at remembering your dreams.

Before going to sleep, tell yourself that you want to remember your dreams. You'll find that doing nothing other than this will greatly improve your dream recall. When you wake up, remain in the position you woke up in, and lie for a few minutes with your eyes closed, thinking about any dream fragments that are in your mind. As you do this, more memories are likely to come back to you. The best time to do this is when you wake up naturally. This is because you normally wake up after a REM cycle if it occurs close to your waking time. When this happens, you're likely to remember the dream.

Research at the Maimonides Medical Center dream laboratory in New York indicates that you can increase the number of precognitive dreams you have by telling yourself before going to sleep that you'll have dreams about the future that night. Malcolm Bessent, one of the subjects in these experiments, was asked to dream about something that would happen on the following day. He managed to do this successfully in fourteen out of sixteen nights (Vaughan, 10).

You can use the same method to encourage angel visitations in your dreams. While lying in bed waiting for sleep, tell yourself that you're going to communicate with an angel, or a specific archangel, in your dreams, and that you'll remember it when you wake up in the morning. Imagine yourself surrounded by a pure white light and gentle, loving angels. You might say to yourself something along the lines of: "Archangel (whichever angel you wish to communicate with), please visit me tonight while I'm asleep and fill my dreams with your insights, guidance, love, and healing energies. Please give me suggestions on how I can become a better person in every area of my life. Please help me resolve (name any problems you have). And please enable me to remember your advice and counsel when I wake up in the morning. Thank you, Archangel (whoever it is), for all your blessings on me and everyone I love. Thank you, thank you, thank you."

Once you've said these words, take a deep breath of pure white, divine light, and exhale slowly. In your mind, see yourself relaxing comfortably, surrounded by pure white light and protected by angels. Relax and allow yourself to drift into sleep.

You need to maintain a regular sleep schedule to ensure you have pleasant dreams that you'll remember when you wake up. The amount of sleep people need varies greatly. Most people need between seven and nine hours of sleep every night. I know someone who never sleeps for more than four hours a night and finds that's all the rest he needs. I also know someone who regularly has ten hours of sleep. Everyone is different.

If you have problems getting to sleep, stay away from caffein-ated drinks and alcohol late in the day. Gentle exercise two or three hours before you go to bed can be helpful. A relaxing, warm bath helps many people fall asleep more easily. I find that reading a book in bed helps me relax enough to fall asleep easily.

LUCID DREAMING

Lucid dreaming occurs when you realize that you're dreaming while you're still experiencing the dream. This means that you're physiologically asleep but at the same time you're consciously aware. In this state, you can direct your dream in any way you wish. You might, for instance, stay in the dream and see what happens. You could just as easily travel to a place you've always wanted to visit or ask a particular archangel to join you for a con-versation. Lucid dreams occur randomly and rarely, usually only a few times in the average person's life.

Fortunately, a number of methods have been developed that enable people to have lucid dreams whenever they want them rather than leaving it up to chance. Some people find they can induce a lucid dream by telling themselves before falling asleep that they'll have a lucid dream that night.

I find it more effective to prepare myself for the lucid dream during the day rather than leaving it until I'm in bed and ready for sleep. The technique is simple and takes about ten minutes.

1. Sit down in a comfortable chair, close your eyes, and take ten slow, deep breaths. Inhale to the count of three, hold it for another three, and then exhale to the count of five.

2. Allow each part of your body to relax as much as possible. Start by relaxing your toes and feet, and work your way up to the top of your head.

3. When you feel completely relaxed, say to yourself: "Tonight, while I'm dreaming, I'll become aware that I'm dreaming, and will be able to direct my dream anywhere I wish. I'll become aware that I'm dreaming, and will be able to direct my dream anywhere I wish." Repeat these words several times. It's important to say these words with conviction, as any doubts will make it that much harder to succeed.

4. When you feel ready, count slowly from one to five, and open your eyes.

5. When you go to bed, remind yourself that you'll be lucid dreaming, and then go to sleep in your usual way.

Another way to encourage lucid dreams is to set your alarm to wake you one hour before your normal time to get up. As soon as you hear it, press the snooze button and allow yourself to drift back to sleep. You'll go straight into the REM state, which is when most lucid dreams occur.

Lucid dreams are always enjoyable, but they're much more beneficial if you have a purpose for the dream. You might, for instance, want to speak to Archangel Ambriel if you're looking for an opportunity to better yourself. Ahead of time, you should decide where you want to meet Ambriel. There's no limit to where you could go, but ideally you should choose a beautiful setting that you know well and can easily visualize in your mind. If you do this, you'll immediately know where to direct the dream to take you once you realize you're dreaming lucidly. You'll also need to know if you'd like Ambriel to be waiting for you at this special place when you arrive, or if you'd rather sit and relax there, and then ask him to join you. Alternatively, you might want Ambriel to appear as soon as you're aware that you're lucid dreaming, so you can travel to your special place together.

If you have a number of specific requirements, write them down and say them in step three of the lucid dream preparation above. In this example, you might say: "Tonight while I'm dreaming, I'll become aware that I'm dreaming and will immediately go to (the place you specified). I'm asking Archangel Ambriel to meet me there, as I have some important questions to ask him about my future. Please meet me there, Archangel Ambriel, as I need help in deciding what to do with my life. Thank you, Archangel Ambriel. I'll see you tonight." Repeat these words several times, and then say them again while lying in bed waiting to fall asleep.

You might be fortunate enough to experience a lucid dream the first time you try it. In my experience that's rare, but with patience and repetition you will soon experience your first lucid dream. After succeeding once, you'll find you can lucid dream almost every time you want to.

CONCLUSION

I hope this book has given you a greater understanding of the archangels, and the work they do for you and for all humanity. I also hope you'll experiment with the different exercises and rituals and gain a closer connection with the angelic realms. I've seen dramatic changes in many people's lives once they started working with angels and am sure this will happen with you, too. The positivity, insight, and love provided by the archangels will help you to develop spiritually, and to live in peace and harmony with others. The archangels will help you reach your goals, no matter how small or large they may be. They'll also help you find your purpose in this incarnation and be more than willing to help you fulfil it. In addition, they'll constantly surround you with divine love.

Several times over the years, people have told me that they believe archangels are too busy to interact with individuals—they're involved in important work related to all of humanity. Archangels are certainly busy, but in my experience they'll respond quickly to your requests. I've called Archangel Michael for help on three occasions, and each time it came instantly. You can and should create a personal connection with the archangels who are important to you. You'll start noticing positive changes in your life as soon as you do. The more you work with them, the more blessings you'll receive, allowing you to become the very best you can be.

Remember, your life can make the angels sing. I wish you great joy, love, and happiness in your quest.

ARCHANGELS FOR DIFFERENT PURPOSES

You can call on any angel you wish when you need help. For instance, many people call on Archangel Michael when they need help. However, there are many other angels you can contact for specific purposes. Here are some of them:

Abundance—Ariel, Barchiel, Raziel, Zadkiel

Acceptance—Zaphkiel

Achievement—Raphael

Addictions (breaking)—Gabriel, Raphael, Uriel

Adversity—Jeremiel, Michael

Affection—Anael, Gabriel

Akashic records (accessing)—Metatron

Alchemy—Raziel, Uriel

Alcoholism—Raphael, Uriel

Anger (controlling)—Uriel, Raguel, Raphael

Animals (protecting and healing)—Ariel, Asariel (especially horses), Orifiel, Sandalphon

Arts (success in)—Gabriel, Jophiel

Astrology—Barbiel (see also the twelve angels of the zodiac)

Beauty—Jophiel

Birds (protection of)—Ariel, Orifiel, Sandalphon

Blessings (to send)—Barchiel, Gabriel

Business (success in)—Anael, Asmodel

Career—Ambriel, Asmodel, Chamuel, Jeremiel

Chakras—Michael

Change—Metatron

Childbirth—Gabriel, Sandalphon, Zuriel

Children—Gabriel, Metatron, Michael, Raphael, Sandalphon, Zaphkiel, Zuriel

Clairvoyance—Asariel, Azrael, Gabriel, Hanael, Jeremiel, Raphael, Raziel

Clarity—Jeremiel, Jophiel, Uriel

Communication—Ambriel, Gabriel, Raphael, Sariel, Zachariel

Compassion—Hanael, Rahmiel, Raphael, Sariel, Zadkiel, Zaphkiel

Conception—Gabriel, Zuriel

Confidence—Adnachiel, Anael, Barchiel, Jehudiel, Metatron, Michael

Contemplation—Cassiel

Cooperation—Raguel

Courage—Camael, Chamuel, Machidiel, Metatron, Michael, Raphael, Samael, Uriel

Creativity—Anael, Asariel, Chamuel, Gabriel, Jophiel, Mizrael, Raphael, Uriel

Depression (overcoming)—Azrael

Divination—Asariel, Gabriel

Divorce—Gabriel, Michael, Raphael, Uriel

Domestic violence (protection from)—Michael, Uriel

Dreams (to encourage)—Gabriel, Jeremiel, Raziel, Remiel

Ecology—Orifiel, Sandalphon

Emotions (controlling)—Gabriel, Jophiel, Muriel

Employment—Anael, Uriel

Empowerment—Raguel

Energy—Michael

Environment—Ariel

Evil (ward off)—Ambriel

Evil eye (preventing)—Ambriel, Sariel

Faith (to encourage)—Michael, Raguel, Raphael

Family—Gabriel, Hanael, Raguel, Verchiel

Fertility—Gabriel

Forgetfulness—Gabriel, Michael

Forgiveness—Chamuel, Jeremiel, Zadkiel, Zaphkiel

Friendship—Anael, Cambiel, Verchiel

Gardening—Ariel, Uriel

Generosity—Sachiel, Zadkiel

Good Fortune—Barchiel, Zadkiel

Grace—Hanael

Gratitude—Gabriel

Grief—Azrael

Guidance—Gabriel, Raphael, Sariel

Happiness—Barchiel, Hanael, Raphael

Harmony (between people)—Cassiel, Hanael, Raguel, Raphael, Remiel, Sahaqiel, Uriel, Zuriel

Hatred (to eliminate)—Gabriel

Healing—Ariel, Gabriel, Michael, Raphael, Sariel, Suriel, Uriel, Zachariel (healing children), Zuriel (mental health)

Health (good)—Raphael, Suriel, Zuriel

Home—Barchiel, Uriel

Honesty—Adnachiel

Hope—Adnachiel, Perpetiel, Sariel

House (to buy)—Uriel

Humor—Barchiel

Impulsiveness—Adnachiel

Independence—Adnachiel

Injury (mental and physical)—Michael, Raphael, Zuriel

Inner peace—Anael, Uriel

Inner strength—Ariel

Inspiration—Metatron

Intellect—Adnachiel, Cambiel, Uriel, Zachariel

Jealousy (to release)—Ariel, Gabriel, Uriel

Joy—Chamuel

Justice—Chamuel, Raguel

Karma—Cassiel, Metatron

Knowledge—Adnachiel, Hamaliel, Raphael, Raziel, Sariel, Uriel

Legal concerns—Chamuel, Sachiel, Zadkiel

Liberty—Jeremiel, Metatron, Michael

Lost items—Chamuel, Michael, Zadkiel

Love—Anael, Asmodel, Chamuel, Gabriel, Hanael, Machidiel, Raguel, Raphael, Sandalphon, Verchiel, Zaphkiel

Loyalty—Raphael

Magic—Ariel, Raziel, Uriel

Manifestation—Ariel, Cambiel, Hanael, Raziel, Uriel

Marriage (harmonious)—Gabriel

Meditation—Raguel, Raphael

Memory—Zachariel, Zadkiel

Mercy—Gabriel

Messages—Gabriel

Miracles—Metatron

Money—Anael, Ariel, Asmodel, Sachiel, Uriel, Zadkiel

Motivation—Metatron, Michael, Verchiel

Music—Gabriel, Sandalphon, Uriel

Natural phenomena—Uriel

Negativity (warding off)—Ambriel, Jophiel

Obedience—Mizrael

Opportunity—Ambriel

Optimism—Adnachiel

Passion (invoke)—Machidiel

Patience—Asmodel, Cassiel, Gabriel, Hamaliel

Peace—Cassiel, Chamuel, Gabriel, Raguel, Remiel, Uriel, Zaphkiel

Persistence—Ariel, Perpetiel, Raguel, Samael

Philosophy—Metatron, Raphael, Uriel

Plant life—Orifiel, Sandalphon

Politics—Sachiel

Prayer—Gabriel, Metatron, Michael, Raphael, Salaphiel, Sandalphon

Pregnancy (protection during)—Gabriel, Sandalphon, Zuriel

Problem solving—Raziel, Zachariel

Procrastination (overcoming)—Michael

Property—Suriel

Prophecy—Jeremiel

Prosperity—Anael, Ariel, Cambiel, Raziel, Sachiel, Uriel, Zadkiel

Protection—Ambriel, Gabriel, Michael, Raphael, Samael, Sidriel, Suriel, Uriel

Psychic skills (development)—Azrael, Gabriel, Hanael, Jeremiel, Raziel, Remiel

Punishment (suitable)—Raguel

Purification—Gabriel, Raphael

Purpose in life—Chamuel, Michael

Recognition—Anael

Reincarnation—Azrael

Relationships—Hanael

Relaxation—Asmodel

Repentance—Michael, Raphael

Responsibility—Ambriel

Science—Cambiel, Hamaliel, Raphael

Secrets—Jeremiel

Self-esteem—Adnachiel, Anael, Jehudiel, Metatron, Michael

Sensitivity—Gabriel

Serenity—Asmodel, Cassiel

Sleep (encourage)—Gabriel

Solutions (to problems)—Michael, Uriel

Soulmate (finding)—Chamuel

Spirituality—Asmodel, Sachiel, Sandalphon

Strength—Camael

Stress—Raphael

Study—Cambiel, Hamaliel, Metatron, Michael, Raphael, Uriel, Zachariel, Zadkiel

Success—Perpetiel, Verchiel

Sympathy—Michael

Tears—Sandalphon

Temperance—Cassiel

Transformation—Cambiel

Travel—Orifiel, Raphael

Trust—Michael, Raguel

Truth—Adnachiel, Jophiel, Michael

Weather—Uriel, Zaphkiel

Wisdom—Metatron, Raphael, Uriel

Worry (eliminating)—Adnachiel, Michael, Raphael

GLOSSARY

Angelophany: The experience of seeing an angel using one or more of the five usual senses. Many instances of this have been recorded in the Bible and other holy texts, as well as in the lives of a number of saints, such as Saint Francis of Assisi who received the stigmata from a seraph. Lorna Byrne, the Irish mystic and author, sees angels every day. There are many accounts of a "mysterious stranger" who appears when someone needs help and then disappears. This is an example of an angel appearing as a human being that the person usually doesn't realize was an angel until afterward.

The Angels of the Presence: (also known as angels of the face) a select group of angels who are close to God. According to the pseudepigraphal book of Jubilees, they were created by God on the first day of Creation. Although Rabbinic lore mentions seventy angels of the presence, traditionally only twelve are recognized: Akatriel, Astanphaeus, Jahoel, Metatron, Michael, Phanuel, Sandalphon, Saraqael, Suriel, Uriel, Yefefiah, and Zagzagel.

Apocrypha: The word "apocrypha" originally denoted works that were too sacred and secret to be available for everyone. Gradually the meaning changed, and today the biblical Apocrypha denote works that are of doubtful authorship and authenticity. The Catholic Church, the Eastern Orthodox Church, the Assyrian Church of the East, and the Oriental Orthodox Church believe that some of the works in the Apocrypha are canonical and include them in their Bibles. However, the Protestant churches either leave them out of the Old Testament entirely or include them in a section called the Apocrypha.

Firmament: The arch or vault over the earth and sky that separates it from heaven. It is mentioned in Genesis 1:6–8: "And God said, Let there be a firmament in the midst of the waters, and let it divide the waters from the waters. And God made the firmament, and divided the waters which were under the firmament from the waters that were above the firmament: and it was so. And God called the firmament Heaven. And the evening and the morning were the second day."

Hierarchy of Angels: Most large organizations have a hierarchical system that ranks its members from the most important to the least important. A hierarchy of angels is a similar arrangement that ranks all the angels in order from the most important to least important. This is a human construct that was considered important for at least fifteen hundred years. It is not considered as seriously today, because most angelologists believe that all angels are of equal importance but perform different tasks.

Merkabah: The Hebrew word for "chariot," this word refers to the chariot-throne of God described in the Bible (Ezekiel 1:4–26). This throne was driven by "four living creatures," each of whom had four wings and four faces, that were of a man, a lion, an ox, and an eagle. According to the Talmud, Archangel Sandalphon stands behind this chariot and Metatron stands beneath its wheels.

Monotheism: The belief that there is only one God. Christianity, Judaism, and Islam are all examples of monotheistic religions.

Polytheism: The belief in a number of gods. Hinduism, Mahayana Buddhism, Santeria, Shinto, and Taoism are examples of polytheistic religions.

Pseudepigrapha: Pseudepigraphal books are works in which the attributed author did not write the book. The term is usually applied to a number of Jewish religious writings written a few hundred years before and after the birth of Christ. The Gospel of Judas is a good example. It consists of a number of conversations between Jesus and Judas Iscariot, but as it was written in the second century CE it could not have been written by Judas. The writings of Pseudo-Dionysius are another example of pseudepigrapha, as the fifth-century writer claimed to be Dionysius the Areopagite, an Athenian who was converted to Christianity by Saint Paul, mentioned in the Acts of the Apostles 17:34. Dionysius the Areopagite lived four hundred years before Pseudo-Dionysius was born.

Schemhamphoras: A group of seventy-two angels who bear the various names of God in the Jewish scriptures. These names are considered to have tremendous power and are often invoked in magic rituals. The most famous "name of power" is the Tetragrammaton, the Jewish sacred name of God. It is usually written as YHVH and pronounced "Jehovah" or "Yahweh."

Stigmata: The appearance of wounds that appear in places on the body that relate to the crucifixion wounds received by Jesus Christ. The person may have from one to five wounds on the hands, feet, head, back, shoulders, or on the side near the heart. St. Francis of Assisi is the first known stigmatic. Other famous people who received the stigmata include Saint Catherine of Siena, Saint Padre Pio, and Therese Neumann.

Bibliography

Agrippa, Henry Cornelius, ed. Donald Tyson. *Three Books of Occult Philosophy*. St. Paul, MN: Llewellyn Publications, 1993.

Ali, Maulana Muhammad. *The Religion of Islam: A Comprehensive Discussion of the Sources, Principles and Practices of Islam*. United Arab Republic: National Publication and Printing House, n.d.

Aquinas, Saint Thomas, trans. James F. Anderson. *Summa Contra Gentiles, Book Two, Creation*. New York: Doubleday and Company, 1956.

Aquinas, Saint Thomas, trans. Ralph McInerny. *Selected Writings*. London: Penguin Books, 1998.

Bailey, Alice A. *A Treatise on the Seven Rays*. New York: Lucis Publishing, 1936.

Barrett, Francis. *The Magus*. Wellingborough, UK: Aquarian Press, 1989. Originally published 1801 by Lackington, Allen and Co (London).

Barrett, W. P. *The Trial of Jeanne D'Arc*. New York: Gotham House, 1932.

Barth, Karl, trans. G.W. Bromiley and R. J. Ehrlich. *Church Dogmatics*, vol. 3, part 3. Edinburgh, Scotland: T & T Clark, 1960.

Bekker, Immanuel, ed. *Chronographia*. Bonn, Germany: Impensis E. Weberi, 1842.

Black, Jonathan. 2013. *The Sacred History: How Angels, Mystics and Higher Intelligence Made Our World*. London: Quercus Books, 2013.

Black, Jeremy, and Anthony Green. *Gods, Demons and Symbols of Ancient Mesopotamia: An Illustrated Dictionary*. London: The British Museum Press, 1992.

Black, Matthew. *The Book of Enoch or I Enoch*. Leiden, Netherlands: E. J. Brill, 1985.

Boudon, Henri-Marie. *Devotion to the Nine Choirs of Holy Angels, Especially to the Angel Guardians*. London: Burns and Oates, 1911.

Brewer, Ebenezer Cobham. *Brewer's Dictionary of Phrase and Fable*. 16th ed. Revised by Adrian Room. London: Cassell & Co, 1999. First published 1870 by Cassel, Petter & Galpin (London).

Bunson, Matthew. *Angels A to Z: A Who's Who of the Heavenly Host*. New York: Crown Trade, 1996.

Byrne, Lorna. *Angels in My Hair: The True Story of a Modern-Day Irish Mystic*. New York: Random House, 2008.

Charles, Robert Henry, ed. *The Apocrypha and Pseudepigrapha of the Old Testament in English*. Oxford, UK: Clarendon Press, 1913. Available online at: http://www.pseudepigrapha.com/jubilees/index.htm

———, trans. *The Book of Jubilees or, The Little Genesis*. London: Society for Promoting Christian Knowledge, 1917. Reprinted 2003 by The Book Tree (San Diego).

———, ed. *The Greek Versions of the Testaments of the Twelve Patriarchs Edited from Nine Mss., Together with the Variants of the*

Armenian and Slavonic Versions and Some Hebrew Fragments. Oxford, UK: Clarendon Press, 1908.

Chase, Steven, trans. *Angelic Spirituality: Medieval Perspectives on the Ways of Angels.* Mahwah, NJ: Paulist Press, 2002.

Conybeare, Frederick C. 1898. "The Testament of Solomon." *Jewish Quarterly Review* 11 (October 1898). http:// www.jstor.org /stable/10.2307/1450398.

Daniell, David. *The Apocrypha: Translated out of the Greek and Latin Tongues Being the Version Set Forth AD 1611 Compared with the Most Ancient Authorities and Revised AD 1894.* London: Folio Society, 2006. Originally published 1895 jointly by Oxford University Press and Cambridge University Press.

Davidson, Gustav. *A Dictionary of Angels Including the Fallen Angels.* New York: The Free Press, 1967.

Echols, Damien. *Angels & Archangels: A Magician's Guide.* Boulder, CO: Sounds True, 2020.

Fretageot, Nora C., and W. V. Mangrum. *Historic New Harmony.* Originally published 1923 by Keller-Crescent Co (Evansville, IN). http://webapp1.dlib.indiana.edu/inauthors /view?docId=VAC2089&doc.view=print.

Ginzberg, Louis, trans. Henrietta Szold. *The Legends of the Jews.* Philadelphia: The Jewish Publication Society of America, 1909, 1910, 1911, 1913, 1925, 1928, and 1938.

Gittings, David. *Spiritual Pilgrimage.* Hereford, UK: New Editions, 1996.

Gray, William G. *The Ladder of Lights.* Cheltenham, UK: Helios Book Service, 1968. Reprinted 1981 by Samuel Weiser (York Beach, ME).

Greer, John Michael. *The New Encyclopedia of the Occult*. St. Paul, MN: Llewellyn Publications, 2003.

Heline, Corinne. *The Blessed Virgin Mary*. New York: New Age Press, 1971.

Humann, Harvey. *The Many Faces of Angels*. Marina del Rey, CA: DeVorss, 1986.

Jameson, Anna. *Legends of the Madonna*. Boston: Houghton Mifflin & Co., 1895.

John of Damascus, trans. E. W. Watson and L. Pullan; eds. Philip Schaff and Henry Wace. *An Exposition of the Orthodox Faith. Book II*. In Nicene and Post-Nicene Fathers, second series, vol. 9. Buffalo, NY: Christian Literature Publishing Company, 1899. Revised and edited 2009 by Kevin Knight, "Church Fathers: An Exposition of the Orthodox Faith, Book II," at New Advent website: http://www.newadvent.org/fathers/33042.htm.

Keck, David. *Angels and Angelology in the Middle Ages*. New York: Oxford University Press, 1998.

Laurence, Richard. *The Book of Enoch the Prophet*. San Diego: Wizard's Bookshelf, 1976.

Leslau, Wolf (editor and translator). *Falasha Anthology*. London: Yale University Press, 1987.

MacGregor, Geddes. *Angels: Ministers of Grace*. New York: Paragon House, 1988.

Mascall, E. L. *The Christian Universe*. New York: Morehouse-Barlow, 1966.

Mathers, S. L. MacGregor (editor and translator). *The Key of Solomon the King*. York Beach, ME: Samuel Weiser, 1989. Originally published 1889 by George Redway (London).

Meyer, Marvin. *The Secret Gospels of Jesus: The Definitive Collection of Gnostic Gospels and Mystical Books about Jesus of Nazareth.* New York: HarperSanFrancisco, 2005.

Meyer, Marvin. *The Nag Hammadi Scriptures: The International Edition.* New York: HarperOne, 2007.

Norwich, John Julius. *Absolute Monarchs: A History of the Papacy.* New York: Random House, 2011.

Oswald, Ian. *Sleep.* Revised ed. Harmondsworth, UK: Penguin, 1970.

Parente, Pascale. *The Angels in Catholic Teaching and Tradition.* Gastonia, NC: Tan Books, 1994.

Possekel, Ute. *Evidence of Greek Philosophical Concepts in the Writings of Ephrem the Syrian.* Leuven, Belgium: Peeters Publishers, 1999.

Pseudo-Dionysius, trans. Colm Luiheid. *Pseudo-Dionysius: The Complete Works.* Mahwah, NJ: Paulist Press, 1987.

Rees, Valery. *From Gabriel to Lucifer: A Cultural History of Angels.* London: Taurus & Company, 2013.

Regardie, Israel. *The Golden Dawn.* 7th ed. Revised and corrected by John Michael Greer. Woodbury, MN: Llewellyn Publications, 2015.

Roberts, Alexander, James Donaldson, Arthur Cleveland Coxe, and Allan Menzies, eds. *The Anti-Nicene Fathers: The Twelve Patriarchs, Excerpts and Epistles, The Clementina, Apocrypha, Decretals, Memoirs of Edessa and Syriac Documents, Remains of the First Ages.* New York: Charles Scribner's Sons, 1886.

Roland, Paul. *Angels: An Introduction to Angelic Guidance, Inspiration, and Love.* London: Judy Piatkus, 1999.

Ronner, John. *Know Your Angels: The Angel Almanac with Biographies of 100 Prominent Angels in Legend and Folklore—and Much More!* Murfreesboro, TN: Mamre Press, 1993.

Savedow, Steve, ed. and trans. *Sepher Raziel Hemelach: The Book of the Angel Raziel.* York Beach, ME: Samuel Weiser, 2000.

Stanford, Peter. *Angels: A Visible and Invisible History.* London, UK: Hodder and Stoughton Limited, 2019.

Vaughan, Alan. "Intuitive Dreaming." *Intuition* 13 (September/October 1996).

Walker, Barbara G. *The Woman's Encyclopedia of Myths and Secrets.* San Francisco: Harper & Row, 1983.

Webster, Richard. *Angels for Beginners: Understand & Connect with Divine Guides & Guardians.* Woodbury, MN: Llewellyn Publications, 2017.

———. *Ritual for Beginners: Simple Ways to Connect to Your Spiritual Side.* Woodbury, MN: Llewellyn Publications, 2016.

———. *Encyclopedia of Angels.* Woodbury, MN: Llewellyn Publications, 2009.

———. *Praying with Angels.* Woodbury, MN: Llewellyn Publications, 2007.

———. *Communicating with the Archangel Uriel for Transformation & Tranquility.* St. Paul, MN: Llewellyn Publications, 2005.

———. *Communicating with the Archangel Gabriel for Inspiration & Reconciliation.* St. Paul, MN: Llewellyn Publications, 2005.

———. *Communicating with the Archangel Raphael for Healing & Creativity.* St. Paul, MN: Llewellyn Publications, 2005.

Webster, Richard. *Communicating with the Archangel Michael for Guidance & Protection*. St. Paul, MN: Llewellyn Publications, 2004.

———. *Spirit Guides and Angel Guardians: Contact Your Invisible Helpers*. St. Paul, MN: Llewellyn Publications, 1998.

INDEX

To Write to the Author

If you wish to contact the author or would like more information about this book, please write to the author in care of Llewellyn Worldwide Ltd. and we will forward your request. Both the author and publisher appreciate hearing from you and learning of your enjoyment of this book and how it has helped you. Llewellyn Worldwide Ltd. cannot guarantee that every letter written to the author can be answered, but all will be forwarded. Please write to:

Richard Webster
℅ Llewellyn Worldwide
2143 Wooddale Drive
Woodbury, MN 55125-2989

Please enclose a self-addressed stamped envelope for reply,
or $1.00 to cover costs. If outside the U.S.A., enclose
an international postal reply coupon.

Many of Llewellyn's authors have websites with additional information and resources. For more information, please visit our website at http://www.llewellyn.com.